Healing the Broken Mind

Healing the Broken Mind

Transforming America's Failed Mental Health System

Timothy A. Kelly

NEW YORK UNIVERSITY PRESS
New York and London

NEW YORK UNIVERSITY PRESS
New York and London
www.nyupress.org

© 2009 by New York University

Library of Congress Cataloging-in-Publication Data
Kelly, Timothy A.
Healing the broken mind : transforming America's failed
mental health system / Timothy A. Kelly.
p. ; cm.
Includes bibliographical references and index.
ISBN-13: 978-0-8147-4812-1 (cl : alk. paper)
ISBN-10: 0-8147-4812-0 (cl : alk. paper)
1. Mental health services—United States. I. Title.
II. Title: Transforming America's failed mental health system.
[DNLM: 1. Mental Health Services—United States. 2. Delivery of Health
Care—United States. 3. Health Care Reform—United States. 4. Health
Policy—United States. WM 30 K295h 2009]
RA790.6.K448   2009
362.10973—dc22   2009005933

New York University Press books are printed on acid-free paper, and their binding materials
are chosen for strength and durability. We strive to use environmentally responsible suppliers
and materials to the greatest extent possible in publishing our books.

Manufactured in the United States of America
10 9 8 7 6 5 4 3 2 1

To my father, Dr. Thomas A. Kelly,
who taught me how to think critically,
and to my mother, Elizabeth Levine Kelly,
who taught me how to love.

Thank you for believing in me so—
for being my #1 fans.

Contents

Acknowledgments

IT TOOK ME over ten years to write this book, which started out as a series of articles after I stepped down as Virginia's ninth mental health commissioner. There are many among my friends, family, students, and colleagues whose support and encouragement kept me going, and I apologize that I cannot list everyone here. Nonetheless I am deeply grateful for each one, as without you this book would not have been written.

I must begin by thanking Broderick Leaks, doctoral student and DePree Fellow, who worked hard to check references, review drafts, and do anything else that was needed as the manuscript progressed. Likewise, I am grateful to my editor, Jennifer Hammer, who patiently shepherded me from first contact to final manuscript, with many great suggestions for improvements. I also wish to thank Dr. Ron Manderscheid and Charles Currie for their feedback on an early draft, while noting that they are not to blame for any questionable opinions that may reside in this book, since those are mine alone. I could never have completed this book without a boss who, like Max DePree (leadership and management expert; see "Leadership Is an Art" at www.depree.org), believes in providing employees whatever they need to succeed. My heartfelt thanks to Walt Wright and the Max DePree Center for Leadership.

I have been privileged to work with hundreds of people over the years who have come to me as a psychologist for help with their mental illness, and it occurs to me that I received more than I gave. I thank each one of you and wish you well from the bottom of my heart. Your trust and honesty, tears and challenges, moved me to become more than I was, even as you grew toward recovery. I hope you will hear the echoes of your voice in these pages, for it is your voice that drove me to write this book.

Without the love and support of my family, I would still be wondering what to do with my instincts toward authorship. My wife, Claire Kelly, my daughters, JoAnn Kelly and Christine Maurer, and my son, Patrick Kelly, all deserve a great portion of any recognition this book may deserve. You believe in me, and I in you, and in that context we are all able to flourish. Solo Gloria Deo.

Abbreviations

ADA	Americans with Disabilities Act
ADHD	attention deficit/hyperactivity disorder
CMHC	community mental health center
DSM-IV	*Diagnostic and Statistical Manual of Mental Disorders, Fourth Edition*
DSM-IV-TR	*Diagnostic and Statistical Manual of Mental Disorders, Fourth Edition, Text Revision*
EAP	Employee Assistance Program
NAMI	National Alliance for the Mentally Ill
NOMs	national outcome measures
OCD	obsessive-compulsive disorder
PACT	Program for Assertive Community Treatment
POMS	Performance Outcomes Measurement System
PTSD	post-traumatic stress disorder
SAMHSA	Substance Abuse and Mental Health Services Administration
SSRI	selective serotonin reuptake inhibitor

1

Men in Diapers

A System in Shambles

A nation's greatness is measured by how it treats its weakest members.
Mahatma Gandhi

America's mental health service delivery system is in shambles . . .
[and] needs dramatic reform.
The President's New Freedom Commission on Mental
Health, *Interim Report to the President* (2002)

MENTAL ILLNESS CAN be frightening both for those who experience
it and for their family and friends, who may try in vain to somehow just
make it all go away. It strikes young and old, rich and poor, Democrat
and Republican alike. Some of our greatest leaders have experienced it,
such as President Lincoln, who struggled with depression. Some of the
most talented artists have experienced it, such as Mozart, who is likely to
have had bipolar disorder. Some of our most brilliant scientists have experienced it, such as Dr. John Nash, the "Beautiful Mind" mathematician.
Nobody is exempt, nobody is somehow "above" being able to become
mentally ill. That may be scary, but it should not keep us from figuring out
what to do about it.

Mental disorders are the leading cause of disability in the United
States and Canada for ages fifteen to forty-four (World Health Organization 2004). Untreated, mental illness can lead to self-destructive impulses
or even death by suicide. Mental illness can be both frightening and debilitating and thus warrants all the help that can reasonably be given so that
those struggling with it may recover (to the extent possible) and take their
place in the home community. Everyone so affected deserves our deepest

sympathy, as well as the most effective treatment society can realistically provide. Even treated and well managed, mental illness is a burden unlike any other. Unlike physical illness or injury it is unseen, yet it mercilessly affects the lives of those who have it in untold ways. Perhaps this is why society has had such difficulty understanding or even recognizing this traumatic reality, much less embracing those so affected. And perhaps this is why policy makers are quick to point out that there are no "votes" to be had in mental health policy, no careers to be made. Thus mental health tends to be the stepchild in policy deliberations—the last to be funded, the first to be passed over. We would rather focus on simpler problems with ready solutions. Simply put, mental illness scares us, so we avoid the topic altogether.

Yet on a deeper level we know (or should know) better. We know that all our neighbors—our fellow citizens—deserve to be treated well, and all the more so when struggling with disabling challenges. We know that there is no such thing as a "throwaway" person. We know that American society will be judged not only by our economic and military might but also by how we treat our most vulnerable members. Accordingly, this book is about recognizing and welcoming our neighbors with mental illness, about understanding their plight and their needs, about what we can do as a nation to make their lives markedly better. It's actually not all that hard to do, except for the resistance to change that is built into all status quo structures. That, of course, is a critical topic and is addressed in the book's last chapter.

I have had the privilege of working in the field of mental health services for over a third of a century in clinical, academic, and governmental positions. From 1994 to 1997 I was appointed by Governor George Allen to serve as commissioner for Virginia's Department of Mental Health, Mental Retardation, and Substance Abuse Services (Kelly 1997), and I have served on various mental health commissions and boards. My experiences as psychologist, as professor, and as commissioner have all led me to the same conclusion: it is time for dramatic change (e.g., Kelly 1997, 2003b, 2007b).[1] It is time to transform the mental health system of care so that persons with even the most serious mental illnesses can regain their place in the home community—so that they can have real homes, fulfilling jobs, and deep relationships.

Others have come to this conclusion as well, and thankfully efforts are being made in that direction. However, resistance to chance is fierce, and it is not yet clear whether America's mental health system will indeed be transformed into an effective and innovative system of care or whether the inevitable pull toward the status quo will win out. This book lays out a road map for achieving lasting transformation. The following are five interrelated recommendations for creating a truly effective mental health system of care:

1. Use results-oriented clinical outcome measures and "evidence-based practices" so as to improve quality of care and accountability.[2]
2. Open the monopolistic state mental health care system to competition and innovation so as to improve treatment choice and effectiveness.
3. Implement "parity" coverage for mental health treatment so as to increase access to care and coverage, per the 2008 parity law.
4. Empower persons with mental illness and their families to have a voice in mental health policy and service delivery so as to ensure consumer input and satisfaction.
5. Win over (or work around) the keepers of the status quo who resist change so as to move ahead toward transformation with all parties at the table.

These five recommendations must be implemented together, as they overlap and interact to create one whole effect—transformation of America's broken mental health care system. The following pages explore and explain each of these recommendations in detail.

Men in Diapers

I was only twelve years old, and Kennedy was president, when I first experienced the state mental health care system. The year was 1963, the place was the Lynchburg Training Center in Virginia, and I was one of dozens of Boy Scouts who were parading through the grounds during the hot summer as a tribute to those unfortunate souls who lived their troubled lives confined there. The training center was practically a city in its own right, located across the river from downtown Lynchburg, housing over five thousand men, women, and children, most with severe and disabling mental retardation. The large brick buildings covering many acres had been built long before air conditioning was available, and most opened onto courtyards surrounded by twelve-foot chain-link fencing that looked very much like a prison's. Our parade route took us along an access road that ran alongside the fenced courtyards.

We marched by the buildings in formation behind each troop's flag, proud to be in uniform and glad to be doing something that was supposed to be good for others. But as we marched on, the chatter and laughter of the scouts slowly died away. There behind the large fences were dozens of men in diapers—in diapers! Many of them had nothing else on, and they hung onto the fence with strange looks as they watched us pass by. Now and again there would be a ruckus of some sort, with yells and grunts and vain attempts to scale the fence, and people in white would rush over to wrestle the diapered men to the ground. Like the other scouts, I knew absolutely nothing about mental retardation or the horrible conditions of places like the Lynchburg Training Center— including the then-current practice of eugenics. But I knew something was terribly wrong with the men behind the tall fences and with the way they were being treated. And I never forgot the sight of grown men in diapers.

Thirty-one years later, in 1994, I entered the grounds of the training center (now renamed the Central Virginia Training Center) for a second time. But this time I was arriving in a state car driven by my staff, and I was there to assess the quality of the treatment program. I had been appointed by the governor to serve as commissioner of Virginia's Department of Mental Health, Mental Retardation, and Substance Abuse Services. And I was eager to see whether the horrors of 1963 had been corrected. The buildings looked much the same, but thankfully the fences had been removed and air conditioning installed. Around the grounds could be seen small groups of "residents" walking from building to building accompanied by their caretakers. Everyone was fully clothed. By outward appearances, life was much improved at the training center.

As commissioner, I was given the red carpet treatment—staff presentations, tours, greeting selected residents, a nice lunch. I was impressed by the dedication of the staff, many of whom worked long hours for low pay in a discouraging environment. I was also impressed by the improvements since 1963. Most of the residents seemed reasonably well cared for, some were productively employed, and none were left to wander untended. But I was troubled by the suspicion that much of what I saw was scripted for me and not necessarily representative of daily life at the training center.

So I came back several weeks later, alone in my state car and completely unannounced. This time I did not park in a space specially prepared for the commissioner. Instead, I simply picked a building at random, parked nearby, and walked in. What I saw confirmed my suspicions. I could see two rooms with six or seven residents in each and two staff chatting amiably together in an adjoining hallway. There was a distinct odor of urine and unwashed clothes and a general unkempt/lazy atmosphere, as if there were nothing to do and nobody cared. No one recognized me or made any effort to "get busy," probably assuming I was just another parent stopping by for a brief visit. As I spoke with the staff and residents, it became clear that this particular building was intended to deal with behavioral problems—residents who had been out of control. That should have meant that these residents would be offered intensive behavior modification treatment until they learned how to appropriately manage anger, frustration, grief, and so on. Instead, they were offered "custodial care," a fancy term for babysitting. I was seething but kept my thoughts to myself.

In subsequent surprise visits to Virginia's fifteen psychiatric facilities I had many such encounters. Once I even walked unannounced into a facility director's office only to find him with his feet literally on the desk, kicking back for a restful afternoon in his comfortable air-conditioned office. (He almost fell over backwards when he saw me.) Worse, I found that custodial care was the norm, not the exception. Time and again I walked unannounced onto a locked psychiatric unit to find the patients overmedicated, slouched on couches, and watching daytime TV together with the staff. This was not just a waste of time and resources, it was unethical and inexcusable. How dare we restrict persons with serious mental illness to locked units only to ignore their pressing need for effective treatment? How dare we offer only custodial care to patients who are vulnerable and completely dependent on whatever is provided? No wonder the mental health care system is described as in a shambles—broken.

This tragic state of affairs was highlighted by a federal commission five years ago. The President's New Freedom Commission on Mental Health issued its interim report in 2002 and its final report in 2003. Here's what they found:

America's mental health service delivery system is in shambles, . . . [and] needs dramatic reform. (2002, i)

For too many Americans with mental illness, the mental health services and supports they need remain fragmented, disconnected and often inadequate, frustrating the opportunity for recovery. Today's mental health care system is a patchwork relic—the result of disjointed reforms and policies. Instead of ready access to care, the system presents barriers that all too often add to the burden of mental illnesses for individuals, their families, and our communities. The time has long since passed for yet another piecemeal approach to mental health reform. Instead, the Commission recommends a fundamental transformation of the nation's approach to mental health care. (2003, 1)

These are stunning admissions for a federal mental health commission to make, and they cry out for a response. Other mental health policy analysts are reaching similar conclusions: that the current system is failing and in need of dramatic overhaul (e.g., Mechanic 2008; Olson 2006). It is time to do the right thing—it is time to transform America's broken mental health system.

Transformation and recovery are what this book is all about—the actions and policies needed to transform mental health services so that persons with mental illness can actually recover and take their place in the home community.[3] There are times when sweeping public policy changes become critical for the welfare of the people, and this is one of those times. It is not an exaggeration to say that the quality of life for millions of Americans suffering from serious mental illness depends upon what our nation does in response to the call for transforming mental health services so as to facilitate recovery. Will there be the usual short-lived fanfare of impressive-sounding state and federal proposals, followed by a few half-hearted initiatives, only to end up with the eventual return to the status quo? Or will this nation roll up its sleeves and do the right thing for the sake of those among us who suffer from the most debilitating of illnesses—mental illness?

The following chapters not only make an appeal for taking up this charge but also present a road map for getting there. Strategic policy proposals are offered for state and federal policy makers, mental health providers, consumers and their family members, and third-party payers (public- and private-sector insurers).[4] For those who are satisfied with the status quo, this book will be of little value. But for those who want to make a difference in the lives of persons with serious mental illness, who want to seize the opportunity afforded by a startlingly honest commission and a time that is ripe for action, read on.

How Bad Is It?

Mental illness is one of the most complex and frustrating health care issues facing society today, and its toll is widespread. Tens of millions of Americans will experience depression, panic attacks, or some other form of mental illness this year. It is estimated that in any given year 26.2 percent of America's adult population (57.7 million people) meet the criteria for a diagnosable mental disorder (Kessler, Chiu, et al. 2005).[5] Countless jobs will be lost and lives put "on hold" as individuals and their families struggle to cope with the chaos and heartbreak of mental illness. Some of those with mental illness will attempt suicide, and, tragically, many of those attempts will be successful. In 2003, 340,000 Americans visited emergency rooms as a result of suicide attempts; over 30,000 of those who attempted suicide died (Substance Abuse and Mental Health Services Administration [SAMHSA] 2006).

Ten years ago, the surgeon general found that over $69 billion was being spent annually in direct costs for mental health services, yet often without the results hoped for (Office of the Surgeon General 1999). Today that figure is much higher, but still results are lacking. America enjoys tremendous prosperity and power, but these have not provided a buffer from mental illness and suicide. How did we get here, and what can be done about it?

A Brief History of Mental Health Treatment

Historically, mental illness has often been misunderstood and feared, and those suffering from it have been stigmatized. In colonial America, persons with mental illness were called lunatics, and their families simply cared for them at home as best they could. Often this meant consigning the suffering individual to a basement or attic or some form of restraint for long periods of time until abnormal behavior subsided. (Unfortunately, this is still the case in many countries throughout the world.) "Professional" treatment consisted of humane custodial care at best, quackery or cruelty at worst. By the nineteenth century, "asylums" were built so that those with mental illness could be cared for outside the home community. The various treatments prescribed in those asylums were largely ineffective. In some cases care was provided by well-meaning staff who treated their patients with compassion and dignity, but in too many other cases poorly trained providers took advantage of their position and cruelly mistreated the patients who were at their mercy. For instance, patients were sometimes found virtually abandoned and chained to walls in small rooms filled with human excrement (Goodwin 1999).

Asylums became known as "mental hospitals" in the early twentieth century, and the numbers of Americans committed within their walls grew substantially, reaching a high of nearly 560,000 in 1955. This rise in demand for inpatient care was driven by several factors, including an aging psychiatric population with nowhere else to go. There were also many World War I and World War II veterans whose combat experiences had triggered chronic mental illness, including what is now referred to as posttraumatic stress disorder (PTSD). Many of those hospitalized suffered from a psychotic disorder: they had lost touch with reality and, in most cases, experienced delusions and/or hallucinations.

In the mid-1950s, the discovery of antipsychotic medications such as Thorazine and Haldol sparked a revolution in inpatient mental health care. These new medications at least partially controlled psychotic symptoms so that, for the first time, persons with schizophrenia and other psychotic disorders were able to be discharged and returned to their home communities. Consequently the population in mental hospitals began to drop dramatically, a movement that continues to this day. The average daily census in America's psychiatric hospitals stood at just over fifty-four thousand in 2000 (SAMHSA 2003). This movement away from hospital care became known as "deinstitutionalization," since hundreds of thousands of people who would otherwise have lived much of their lives in psychiatric institutions were able to return to their home communities. The initial hope was that antipsychotic medication would do for mental illness what penicillin did for infections—provide a cure. Unfortunately, pharmaceutical treatment and deinstitutionalization, while helpful, also elicited a new set of problems. The medications controlled psychotic symptoms to some extent, and for some patients the results were wonderful. But many others found that they triggered severe side effects such as tardive dyskinesia (unstoppable and often embarrassing repetitive motions) and left the patient feeling overtranquilized, emotionally stunted, and interpersonally dysfunctional.

Moreover, deinstitutionalization led to a predictable need to provide effective outpatient treatment and services so that the many patients discharged from psychiatric facilities could find the support and services required to succeed in their home communities. In response to this need, a complementary revolution in community mental health care soon developed—the community mental health center (CMHC) movement. The laudable goal was to provide outpatient services so that persons with serious mental illness (including those discharged from hospitals) could receive the care needed to live successfully in their home communities. CMHCs were launched with federal funding in the 1960s, and currently many dedicated and talented providers offer excellent care in today's CMHCs. However, the CMHC system is now too often functioning as a dispenser of ineffective or insufficient status quo services, without the full range of community supports and innovative treatments needed to provide effective care. Consequently it is not unusual for a person with serious mental illness to be discharged from a psychiatric hospital, return to his or her local CMHC, get rapidly worse because of ineffective care, and eventually end up rehospitalized. This vicious cycle is emblematic of a broken system of care and serves the best interests of no one.

The vicious cycle also contributes to a rising population of the "homeless mentally ill" and seems to provide evidence for the claim that deinstitutionalization has failed. In fact both revolutions, deinstitutionalization and community mental health care, are examples of well-intentioned public policy poorly implemented. Most persons with serious mental illness need not live their lives institutionalized and can recover enough to live successfully in their home community. So the goal of discharging patients as soon as possible from inpatient care is appropriate and ethical. However, for that to work, a whole new array of home- and community-based services must be put in place. Otherwise, patients are sent home to predictable deterioration and, eventually, to readmission. The vicious cycle exists not because deinstitutionalization is the wrong policy but because sufficient and effective community services are not available. The one without the other is a recipe for disaster. The mental health care system is well intentioned but broken and must be transformed.

What Is Mental Illness?

It is important to clarify terms before proceeding, yet mental illness is surprisingly difficult to define. Unlike communicable physical illness, there is no pathogen—no viral or bacterial infection—that can be readily identified and treated. The affected organ is, of course, the brain, and many mental illnesses are associated with changes in brain chemistry. But the etiology, or cause, of mental illness remains largely unknown and there are many competing definitions of the term. To clarify the definition, it is helpful to appeal to the "biopsychosocial" model used by social scientists, as well as two other well-regarded definitions.

Most behavioral scientists embrace the biopsychosocial model (Engel 1977), which means that a given mental illness (such as schizophrenia or depression) may have several components—biological, psychological, and social. The biological component refers to the fact that some persons are born with a vulnerability to specific illnesses (both physical and mental). Such persons are "genetically predisposed," meaning that statistically they are more likely to develop a given illness than the average person. So, for instance, the child of a person with schizophrenia is more likely than others to have inherited the genetic structure that is associated with this disorder. That does not mean for certain that the child will develop schizophrenia, but it does mean that he or she is more at risk biologically. Likewise, a child may inherit a genetically driven tendency to withdraw from others socially, which makes him or her more likely to experience depression later in life (Tan and Ortberg 2004).

The psychological component refers to the fact that certain patterns of thinking or feeling are associated with mental illness. For instance, a person who tends to draw negative conclusions about self despite positive evidence to the contrary is more likely to experience depression (J. Beck 1995; Tan and Ortberg 2004). The social component refers to the stressful or traumatic experience that often triggers mental illness. For instance, depression can be triggered by a significant loss such as the breakup of a long-standing relationship or the loss of a job (Tan and Ortberg 2004). The biopsychosocial model of mental illness has proven helpful for research and treatment and provides a useful conceptual framework for defining mental illness as well.

The surgeon general's well-regarded report on mental health defines mental illness as "diagnosable mental disorders . . . characterized by alterations in thinking, mood, or behavior . . . associated with distress and/ or impaired functioning" (Office of the Surgeon General 1999). In this definition, *diagnosable* is the operative word, and it is what distinguishes mental illness from other, less serious problems such as adjustment to life difficulties. Saying that mental illness is "diagnosable" means that a person's symptoms meet the criteria specified in the *Diagnostic and Statistical Manual of Mental Disorders, Fourth Edition, Text Revision* (*DSM-IV-TR;* American Psychiatric Association 2000). The *DSM-IV,* published by the

American Psychiatric Association, lists observable or reportable criteria for every recognized classification of mental illness. For instance, to be diagnosed as having depression an individual would have to have experienced, for a period of time, at least five of nine specific symptoms (e.g., sad mood, sleep disturbance, low energy, difficulty concentrating, and thoughts of self-harm). Since both public and private health insurers typically require *DSM-IV* diagnoses to cover treatment for mental illness, this manual has come to play a critical role in mental health care treatment and policy.

The second well-regarded definition comes from the National Alliance for the Mentally Ill (NAMI). NAMI is the nation's largest mental health advocacy organization, with chapters in every state, and exists to support individuals and families struggling with mental illness.[6] This organization is very active in the arena of mental health policy at both the state and federal levels, correctly recognizing that such policies greatly affect the quality of life of those with mental illness. NAMI tends to focus on "serious mental illness" and works from the premise that persons with serious mental illnesses require a combination of medication, psychotherapy, and community support services in order to recover. NAMI (2008) defines mental illnesses as "a disorder of the brain that disrupts a person's thinking, feeling, moods, ability to relate to others, and daily functioning . . . [and] often result in a diminished capacity for coping with the ordinary demands of life."

I believe that these two definitions are complementary and fit well within the framework of the biopsychosocial model. Consequently, throughout this book, I will use the following definition of mental illness, which draws on all three perspectives: "Mental illness is a biopsychosocial brain disorder characterized by dysfunctional thoughts, feelings, and/or behaviors that meet *DSM-IV* diagnostic criteria."

What Is Serious Mental Illness?

A working definition of mental illness provides at least a starting point for developing mental health policy. For instance, it clarifies the difference between genuine mental illness and general "life difficulties," such as feeling stressed out or somewhat down, since mental illness must be formally diagnosable by the *DSM-IV*. But that leads logically to an important question: Is every diagnostic category listed in the *DSM-IV* equally burdensome to the individual and thus equally deserving of priority attention? Some would argue yes and feel that to leave out any category of mental illness in policy discussions is a great mistake. Others (such as NAMI) argue that it makes more sense to focus attention and resources on a priority basis on "serious mental illness," which by definition is more debilitating than the milder forms of mental illness included in the *DSM-IV.*

The trouble is that the *DSM-IV* is like a dictionary, intended to be broad and comprehensive and thus inclusive of every possible category of mental illness regardless of severity. It is an attempt to catalog and classify *all* pathological psychological experiences outside the "norm." Accordingly, it includes forms of mental illness that do not warrant the same level of attention as, say, schizophrenia or major depression. Pathological deviations from the norm included in the *DSM-IV* range from mild cases of simple caffeine intoxication to potentially suicidal cases of chronic major depression. This poses a challenge for insurers, whether private or governmental, who must set parameters for coverage eligibility. Should all 297 categories of mental illness listed in the *DSM-IV* be equally covered, or should some be prioritized over others?

To answer the question, consider the contrast mentioned above—caffeine intoxication versus chronic major depression. Not surprisingly, caffeine intoxication is caused by the ingestion of excessive amounts of caffeine, which results in symptoms such as restlessness, insomnia, and nervousness. Although many a college student has experienced the results of a caffeine overdose while studying for exams, it is unlikely that this form of mental illness is serious enough to warrant priority treatment. Chronic major depression, on the other hand, can be debilitating in the extreme and frequently includes suicidal thoughts or actions. Untreated, it can literally end in death. More often, it leads to a life of increasing dysfunction at home, at school, or in the workplace. It is clear that this form of mental illness is indeed serious enough to warrant priority treatment and that effective care should be made available through private insurance, the public mental health care system, or both.

Mental health researchers and policy makers have labored for some time to define serious mental illness in order to distinguish it from less severe forms of dysfunction. Serious mental illness is based on two factors— diagnosis (severe categories) and level of functioning (highly debilitating). A consensus definition has yet to emerge, but the surgeon general's mental health report states that "this category includes schizophrenia, bipolar disorder, other severe forms of depression, panic disorder, and obsessive-compulsive disorder" (Office of the Surgeon General 1999, 46).[7] The report's definition provides a useful starting point since it includes psychotic disorders, which are the most severe mental illnesses, and mood and anxiety disorders, which are the most common mental illnesses. However, it leaves out childhood disorders such as attention deficit disorder, eating disorders, and substance use disorders. Disorders in these categories are also common and debilitating. In fact, many who suffer from a mental illness also struggle with substance use disorders. Accordingly, I believe that serious mental illness should include six categories of mental disorders:

1. Psychotic disorders (e.g., schizophrenia)
2. Mood disorders (e.g., bipolar disorder, major depression)
3. Anxiety disorders (e.g., panic disorder)
4. Childhood disorders (e.g., attention deficit/hyperactivity disorder)
5. Eating disorders (e.g., anorexia)
6. Substance use disorders (e.g., alcohol dependence)

Insurance coverage should vary for specific mental disorders according to the severity of the illness. For instance, under "childhood disorders" Tourette's disorder (uncontrollable and highly disruptive tics) should be included in every plan given its severity. But mathematics disorder (lower than expected mathematical ability) could be in the "uncovered" category, except perhaps for the most extensive and expensive coverage packages intended to include all possible diagnoses.

As mentioned above, serious mental illness is based not only on diagnosis but also on level of functioning. In other words, a person experiencing a serious mental illness not only will meet the criteria for a disorder in one of the six categories listed but also will have significant difficulty in functioning at home, work, or school. For example, this may involve weeping uncontrollably throughout the day (depression), experiencing heart attack–simulating panic when with others (agoraphobia), or hearing viciously accusing voices that are not there (schizophrenia). Such experiences make it impossible to function well, which is part of the grim reality of serious mental illness. In sum, the most serious mental disorders are recognized by a combination of diagnosis and functionality. Such disorders will always involve a severe diagnosis and a significantly compromised level of functioning.

Although the prevalence of serious mental illness is hard to determine, especially since there is no consensus on which diagnoses to include, it is estimated that about 6 percent of the U.S. adult population (13.2 million people) suffer from a serious mental disorder (Kessler, Chiu, et al. 2005).

Serious Mental Illness: Symptoms and Treatment

As described above, serious mental illness involves six categories of mental disorders, including schizophrenia and major depression. Unfortunately, there is much confusion both about mental illness in general and about specific disorders, as indicated by questions such as "Is mental illness caused by poor parenting?" or "Can mental illness be caught by spending time with a person suffering from serious mental illness?" The answer to both questions is "no." Although poor parenting can, of course, contribute to a child's problems, the biopsychosocial model is based on the premise that mental illness is caused by multiple factors. Many people from good families become mentally ill, and many of those from dysfunctional families do not. And, of course, since mental illness does not involve a viral or bacterial infection it cannot be "caught."

Anyone experiencing serious mental illness without the benefit of effective treatment can easily get to the point where he or she is simply unable to function in society. The sadness, anxiety, and uncontrollable behaviors that are part of serious mental illness—and, in the case of schizophrenia or other psychotic disorders, the delusions and hallucinations—can easily become too much for a person to bear. However, when provided with effective treatment, the majority of persons with serious mental illness can live a healthy, productive life in their home community. Thus effective care benefits not only the individual in need but the community as well, which would otherwise lose a valuable member.

Even from a purely pragmatic and financial perspective it makes sense to help persons with serious mental illness early on, before a crisis point is reached. Prevention and early intervention programs, such as support groups and counseling offered in schools, are much less expensive than the types of services provided post crisis—such as hospitalization and incarceration.

It is important to understand something of what a person with serious mental illness experiences so as to fully appreciate the imperative to transform America's broken mental health care system. The reader who is already familiar with the clinical aspects of mental illness and its treatment may want to skip the following sections. But for the sake of those not familiar with the realities of serious mental illness, what follows is a brief profile of some of the major disorders. The reader should remember that this sketch is simply a snapshot of some of the more common disorders in the six categories defined as constituting serious mental illness. For a more complete overview of emotional disorders, see *Psychopathology: History, Diagnosis, and Empirical Foundations* (Craighead, Miklowitz, and Craighead 2008).

Schizophrenia: A Psychotic Disorder

Schizophrenia is perhaps both the most debilitating and most misunderstood of the serious mental illnesses. The misuse of the term *schizophrenic* to apply to a Jekyll-and-Hyde personality just adds to the confusion. Schizophrenia does *not* mean "split personality" or "multiple personality," even though the term, coined by Swiss psychiatrist Eugen Bleuler in 1911, does literally mean "split mind." The "split" referenced by Bleuler is a division between experiences and feelings, or between thoughts and reality. Persons with schizophrenia may react in a bizarre manner to a normal social situation because their thoughts or feelings are not corresponding to what is actually happening around them. Individuals with schizophrenia are considered psychotic, meaning that they have lost touch with reality. They may see and hear things that are not there, or they may have bizarre delusions that seem absolutely real to them.

Schizophrenia seems to strike out of the blue, typically in late adolescence or early adulthood. It can affect the best and brightest and often lasts a lifetime. It is not possible to describe schizophrenia without recognizing the heartbreak that this disorder entails. The tragedy of schizophrenia was well portrayed in *A Beautiful Mind*, a movie about the life of Nobel Prize winner John Nash Jr. As demonstrated in Nash's case, some persons are born with a genetic vulnerability to this disorder. (Nash's son also has schizophrenia.) Approximately 1.1 percent of the population (2.4 million adults) develops schizophrenia, a percentage that is fairly stable across cultures (Gottesman 1991).

There are five types of this disorder, but perhaps the best known is paranoid schizophrenia. This often involves unrelenting and extreme delusions of persecution or threat and the belief that others are "out to get you." Those who are actively experiencing paranoid schizophrenia are at greater risk of hurting themselves or others if they do not receive treatment. However, with effective treatment, with symptoms under control, and with good social support the risk for harm is typically no greater or less than for anyone else.

The symptoms of schizophrenia vary greatly but can involve auditory or even visual hallucinations that are often threatening and frightening, such as hearing voices or seeing demonic figures. Bizarre delusions and peculiar behavior are common experiences for persons with schizophrenia, who may believe, for example, that they are receiving messages from a dead person or from the CIA. The emotional response of persons with schizophrenia is often completely unrelated to their actual situation. For example, one may laugh after hearing of the death of a loved one, while another may show no feelings at all. Of course, these symptoms result in dramatic dysfunction at work, home, or school. The tragedy of this disorder is compounded by the fact that a person with schizophrenia may have times of normality interspersed with periods of delusion or hallucination. This often confuses and gives false hope to the individual, as well as to friends and family.

Until the 1990s, treatment for schizophrenia relied almost solely on conventional antipsychotic medication that decreased delusions and hallucinations to the point where a person with schizophrenia could again function at home and at work. However, these medications (e.g., Thorazine and Haldol) came with the risk of serious side effects such as tardive dyskinesia.[8] Additionally, heavy dosages of these medications often left the patient feeling overmedicated, as if even normal thoughts and feelings were restricted by an invisible barrier. Consequently, a person with schizophrenia had to make the difficult choice between continuing to endure psychosis or risking the downside of conventional antipsychotic medications.

More recently, new "atypical" antipsychotic medications (e.g., Clozaril, Risperdal, Zyprexa, Seroquel, Abilify, and Invega) were developed that seemed capable of reducing the effects of psychosis with minimal risk of serious side effects (Comer 2004, 473). However, research has determined that these medications also come with significant risk of unintended side effects, such as obesity, diabetes, or, in the case of Clozaril, agranulocytosis (decreased white blood cell count). Additionally, there is some indication that conventional antipsychotic medications can be equally effective, and less likely to trigger side effects, if dosage is kept to a minimum and patients' reactions are carefully monitored (McEvoy et al. 2006; Stroup et al. 2006).

Antipsychotic medications, carefully matched to the patient and properly dosed, can accomplish wonders. In fact, as commissioner I personally witnessed many "Clozaril miracles"—patients who had not responded to any of the traditional medications for many years, yet "came back" to reality and eventually to their home community through the use of Clozaril.

Medication alone is not sufficient, however. Once medication has taken effect, treatment should expand to include supportive therapy for the individual and his or her family, as well as vocational and psychoso-cial rehabilitation if needed. Even with effective treatment, schizophrenia is a heavy burden to bear. The individual, and often family members as well, need help managing the challenges posed by ongoing medication, by symptoms when they appear, or by misunderstanding in the home or workplace. With effective treatment and rehabilitative supports in place, a person with schizophrenia can do well at home and at work and move to-ward recovery. Thankfully there are many cases demonstrating just that— yet there need to be more.

Mood Disorders: Major Depressive Disorder and Bipolar Disorder

Mood disorder is the term used in the *DSM-IV* for mental disorders char-acterized by depression, mania, or both. Major depression and bipolar (manic-depressive) disorder involve much more than simple mood swings from sadness to elation, which are simply part of normal experiences.

Major Depressive Disorder

Major depressive disorder is the most common mental health diagnosis and is the leading cause of disability in the United States for ages fifteen to forty-four (World Health Organization 2004). Worldwide, it ranks among the top ten causes of all disabilities (Murray and Lopez 1996). Major depres-sive disorder affects approximately 6.7 percent of adults (14.74 million) in a given year (Kessler, Chiu, et al. 2005), and affects a significant portion of America's children and adolescents as well (SAMHSA 2007). A person with depression experiences, for a sustained period, symptoms such as sadness and crying, sleep disturbance, loss of energy and interest, loss of appetite, difficulty concentrating, and thoughts of self-harm. Depression can be trig-gered by a psychosocial stressor such as a loss (e.g., the end of a relationship, death of a spouse, or loss of a job) that constitutes the social component in the biopsychosocial model. In addition, depression often involves changes in brain chemistry (the biological component) and negative thought pat-terns (the psychological component). The difference between diagnosable depression and "feeling down" is a matter of severity, duration, and impair-ment. Anyone can feel down for a day or so, but depression can last months, immobilize a person, and lead to suicide. Tragically, about 10 percent of persons with the most serious forms of depression (those who typically seek hospitalization) eventually attempt suicide (SAMHSA 2006).

Depression can be effectively treated with psychotherapy, antide-pressants, or a combination of both. There are three major classes of antidepressants, but the most frequently used are known as the "SSRI" (selective serotonin reuptake inhibitor) antidepressants, which include Prozac and Zoloft (Comer 2004). The primary function of these medications is to increase the active amount of a brain neurotransmitter, serotonin, which in turn elevates an individual's mood. With fewer side effects and greater effectiveness than the older antidepressants, these medications have become common. Currently, tens of millions of Americans are taking antidepressants, most of which are prescribed (and too often overprescribed) by a general practitioner rather than by a psychiatrist.

Although these medications are useful in many cases, there is a tendency for both patients and providers to see them as a quick fix—the solution to depression in a pill. Consequently we as a society have become overdependent on antidepressants, often prescribing or renewing them without question when a careful assessment would suggest otherwise. As a practicing psychologist I have seen many patients take SSRI antidepressants for years, assuming it will brighten their mood and ward off depression indefinitely. In reality, many medications when overused tend to lose their effectiveness as tolerance develops. Further, for some persons SSRI antidepressants can increase the likelihood of self-harm by providing energy for action before the depression has lifted. Such medications are best used cautiously and in moderation, as an adjunct to other treatment (Healy 2004: Miranda, Chung, and Green 2003).

Several mainstream psychotherapies have been shown to be as effective in treating depression as SSRI medications and in some cases longer-lasting (Comer 2004). Of these, cognitive-behavioral psychotherapy (which deals with negative thought patterns) and interpersonal psychotherapy (which focuses on relationships) have been shown to be particularly helpful. In some cases, a combination of psychotherapy and a course of medication constitutes the most effective treatment approach. Thankfully, the majority of persons suffering from major depression, about 60 percent, respond well to appropriate treatment (Comer 2004).

Bipolar Disorder
Bipolar disorder, formerly called manic-depressive disorder, involves experiencing a manic episode (an abnormally elevated, expansive, or irritable mood) as well as depression. The manic mood is accompanied by symptoms that could include grandiosity, decreased need for sleep, flight of ideas, pressured speech (speaking rapidly and excitedly without pause),

and, in some cases, self-destructive activities such as sexual indiscretions or buying sprees. Extreme cases can include psychotic symptoms, such as delusions or auditory hallucinations. Like depression, a manic episode can be triggered by a psychosocial stressor. The manic episode can last for minutes or for days and often either follows or precedes a depressive episode. The cycle from depression to mania and back can occur rapidly within a day or slowly over weeks. Approximately 2.6 percent of adults (5.7 million) and 1.1 percent of children and adolescents (275,000) suffer from bipolar disorder (Kessler, Chiu, et al. 2005; Office of the Surgeon General 1999). Untreated, this disorder can quickly ruin lives, as a person experiencing mania may behave in such a way as to hurt family, property, employment, or self. Self-destructive behaviors, including suicide attempts, are not uncommon.

Treatment for bipolar disorder usually begins with medication to stabilize the manic mood swings. Throughout the years, lithium has been the most frequently prescribed and most effective medication for this disorder, with minimal side effects for many. Recently, new medications that were originally developed as anticonvulsants (e.g., Tegretol and Depakote) have been found to be particularly effective in treating bipolar disorder, especially for those who do not respond to lithium (National Institute of Mental Health 2000). In my clinical experience, I have found that it is not unusual for a person with severe bipolar disorder to be taking a number of medications—for example, one for mania, another for depression, and perhaps a third to control side effects from the first two. Appropriate medication is of course critical, but there seems to be a tendency to overmedicate and to ignore the need for adjunctive psychotherapy. Supportive, practical psychotherapy is usually necessary to help a person cope with this disorder, including learning new strategies for managing bipolar experiences.

Anxiety Disorders: Panic Attacks, Obsessive-Compulsive Disorder, and Post-traumatic Stress Disorder

Anxiety disorders involve extreme experiences of anxiety that can debilitate an individual. These disorders are very different from experiencing fear in the face of danger, worrying about life's concerns, or feeling stress under pressure—all of which are part of the normal human experience. An anxiety disorder can lead to wild panic, bizarre obsessive/compulsive behaviors (e.g., washing one's hands hourly or constantly checking locked doors), or terrifying reexperiences of a trauma such as rape.

Panic Disorder

Panic attacks usually involve a gut-wrenching, overwhelming sense of fear—often including the belief that one is "going crazy" or about to die. Accompanying this fear are symptoms that may include a racing heart rate, sweating and trembling, shortness of breath, or hot flashes. The attack usually comes on suddenly and builds to a crescendo within ten to fifteen minutes. By then, it is not unusual for the person who is having the attack to lose control (e.g., to run out of a building, to scream, or to cry hysterically). All of this is very costly on the individual, both physically and emotionally. Panic attacks are associated with other anxiety disorders such as phobias (an inordinate fear of an object or situation) and agoraphobia (fear of public settings). In both cases the person engages in avoidant behavior—either of objects or of being in public—to keep from having a panic attack. A person struggling with agoraphobia, for example, may stay at home because that's the only way to ensure that he or she will not end up having a panic attack. Needless to say, these attacks and the behaviors they elicit can be highly disruptive at home, at school, or on the job. Approximately 2.7 percent of adults (6 million) currently experience severe panic attacks and their associated disorders (National Institute of Mental Health 2007). About 13 percent of children and adolescents (3.25 million) experience some level of anxiety-related difficulty or disorder (SAMHSA 2003a).

Obsessive-Compulsive Disorder

Obsessive-compulsive disorder (OCD) consists of two components: obsessive thoughts and compulsive behaviors. An obsessive thought is an abhorrent thought, image, or impulse that invades a person's consciousness and cannot be "turned off." A compulsive behavior is a repetitive, unwanted action that cannot be resisted. The two usually go hand in hand. For instance, Howard Hughes, the billionaire, who suffered from obsessive-compulsive disorder during the last half of his life, was irrationally concerned about germs. He could not stop thinking about infection, so he developed elaborate and bizarre routines such as opening doors with his feet to avoid germs. This was depicted well in the movie *The Aviator* (2004), which showed how a person such as Hughes can be very accomplished and intelligent and still suffer greatly from OCD. Severe OCD, untreated, can be quite debilitating, as individuals may spend much of their time pursuing compulsive, irrational behaviors. Approximately 1.0 percent of adults (2.2 million) experience some level of OCD (Kessler, Chiu, et al.

2005). It is estimated that between 0.2 and 0.8 percent of children, and up to 2 percent of adolescents suffer from some level of OCD-related difficulty or disorder (Office of the Surgeon General 1999).

Post-traumatic Stress Disorder

Post-traumatic stress disorder (PTSD) was officially recognized as a mental disorder in 1980, largely in response to Vietnam War veterans who were experiencing debilitating symptoms. Formerly, similar symptoms that affected World War II veterans were diagnosed as "combat fatigue," and World War I veterans were declared to be suffering from "shell shock." But PTSD is not limited to war trauma. It can be caused by exposure to any horrifying, traumatic stressor, including combat, violent assault (e.g., rape), kidnapping, torture, a severe auto accident, or a major natural disaster. Symptoms include reexperiencing the trauma in nightmares or flashbacks, sometimes many years after its original occurrence. Because these experiences are often triggered by something reminiscent of the initial event, persons with PTSD may go to great lengths to avoid places or reminders of their trauma. If despite their best efforts the trauma is invoked, they may suddenly and unexpectedly reexperience the full anxiety and horror of the original event through a flashback. Such experiences can be truly debilitating and unnerving. This mental disorder is somewhat unique in that its cause (the trauma) is known. What is not known is why some individuals develop PTSD while others who experienced the same trauma do not. About 19 percent of Vietnam War veterans experienced PTSD at some point after the war (Dohrenwend et al. 2006), although one study found the rate for those exposed to heavy combat much higher (36 percent; Kulka et al. 1988). There is no reason to believe that veterans returning from Iraq and Afghanistan will not suffer similar rates. Overall, 3.5 percent of America's adult population (7.7 million) have PTSD in a given year (Kessler, Chiu, et al. 2005).

Treatment for anxiety disorders often involves both medication and psychotherapy. Some SSRI antidepressants have proven to be helpful in some cases for both OCD and panic attacks. Panic attacks are also treated with antianxiety medication known as benzodiazepines (e.g., Klonopin and Valium), though these can become addictive. A newer medication, BuSpar, may be helpful in some cases in providing a nonaddictive alternative for reducing general anxiety (Comer 2004). Many persons who are dealing with a severe anxiety disorder benefit not only from medication but also from psychotherapy. Psychotherapy may be supportive and practical, focusing on strategies for managing anxiety such as relaxation techniques: it may be cognitive-behavioral, focusing on replacing anxious thought patterns, or it may be insight oriented, helping an individual to work through his or her feelings and defuse the impact of the initial trauma. A more recently developed form of brief psychotherapy, eye movement desensitization and reprocessing (EMDR), has demonstrated notable effectiveness in treating PTSD (Craighead, Miklowitz, and Craighead 2008). This involves triggering left-right eye movement, or tapping left-right on shoulders, while the patient recounts and reprocesses the trauma experience and its meaning.

A large number of military personnel returning from the wars in Iraq and Afghanistan suffer from PTSD or other stress-related disorders. For that reason, the Pentagon announced in August 2008 a $300 million program on research and treatment for PTSD and traumatic brain injury. This unprecedented effort will likely revolutionize our understanding of how PTSD works (etiology and course) and lead to new and more effective treatments for veterans and civilians alike suffering from anxiety disorders. Although anxiety disorders rarely disappear altogether, with effective evidence-based treatment those suffering from them can usually minimize and manage their symptoms and return to a fully functioning lifestyle.[9]

Attention Deficit/Hyperactivity Disorder: Typically, a Childhood Disorder

Attention deficit/hyperactivity disorder (ADHD) is the most commonly diagnosed behavioral disorder of childhood, although it can also be found among adults. Research shows that it is four times more common among boys than girls and that it affects approximately 5 percent of the child and adolescent population (1.25 million) (Office of the Surgeon General 1999). ADHD has generated a good deal of controversy—especially among parents who feel that the diagnosis and medication are too readily given in order to calm disruptive children. There is, in fact, evidence to warrant more research on whether the diagnosis may at times be given too freely to children who meet only some of the actual criteria for ADHD in an effort to control poor behavior (Office of the Surgeon General 1999). Mild ADHD symptoms in children who are somewhat prone to disruptive behavior or inattention may often best be dealt with through parental/teacher attention and special tutoring rather than medication. However, severe ADHD involves measurable dysfunction in the brain's ability to process information and cannot be addressed with tutoring alone. Children suffering from severe ADHD are simply unable to perform at home or at school and are very much in need of effective treatment, which may include medication.

While children tend to be the subject of most discussions of ADHD, it is important to recognize that the malady also affects many adults, who often suffer more damaging effects than children. ADHD affects an estimated 4.1 percent of those aged eighteen to forty-four (Kessler, Chiu, et al. 2005). Adults with ADHD may have trouble holding down a job or managing their finances. Forming and maintaining relationships can also be difficult, leading to increased loss and stress in their lives. Both adolescents and adults with untreated ADHD are at increased risk for substance abuse and dangerous impulsivity, a combination that sometimes results in tragedies such as automobile accidents and acts of violence (SAMHSA 2003a). ADHD is characterized by two sets of symptoms: inattention and hyperactivity. Although any child can, of course, be inattentive and hyperactive at times—especially when upset—the cluster of symptoms for ADHD goes far beyond the normal range of behavior. For instance, a child with severe ADHD may be always talking and moving around, unorganized, inattentive, and unable to focus in on or complete tasks at school or home. Whereas a few of these behaviors are to be expected from any child now and again, it is the sum of all these behaviors exhibited most of the time that marks severe ADHD.

Treatment for ADHD usually involves both medication and behavioral therapy. The medications—"psychostimulants" including Ritalin and Adderall—arouse or stimulate brain regions that are responsible for directing attention and inhibiting impulses. While it may seem counterintuitive that an energizing medication would help to treat a hyperactive disorder, the results have clearly been positive. At least 80 percent of children with ADHD respond well to psychostimulants (Comer 2004). Although the actual mechanism of improvement is not known, it has been hypothesized that a stimulant may improve the ability of a child with ADHD to focus more effectively on one thing at a time by "arousing" his or her interest level. Behavioral therapy is often required as a complement to medication to help parents and teachers establish structure in the child's life and reinforce rewards and consequences for actions. Otherwise, dysfunctional learned behaviors (bad habits) can deter improvement, even with successful medication.

Anorexia Nervosa: An Eating Disorder

Anorexia nervosa is an eating disorder characterized by refusal to eat what is required to maintain a minimally normal body weight. Those suffering from this disorder are inordinately afraid of gaining weight and exhibit a significant disturbance in perception of the shape or size of their body. For instance, an individual may be emaciated, yet see an overweight body in the mirror. Females account for more than 90 percent of all cases. Anorexia nervosa is a potentially life-threatening disorder, since those who experience it are in jeopardy of literally starving themselves to death. They may also die from suicide or from starvation complications such as electrolyte imbalance. Tragically, the long-term mortality rate among persons with the most severe cases of anorexia (i.e., those who are hospitalized at some point) is over 10 percent. Treatment for anorexia nervosa can involve medication, psychotherapy, or both. Psychotherapy can be essential, given the "therapeutic relationship" in which a caring professional helps monitor and work against starvation. Unfortunately, to date, this disorder has proven to be particularly difficult to treat effectively. Many who suffer from anorexia find themselves going from treatment to treatment without recovering their ability to function well on a daily basis. This is one example of a mental disorder that cries out for innovative treatments to be developed and tested.

Substance Use Disorders

There is a good deal of discussion among third-party payers as to whether substance abuse disorders should be covered with other mental illnesses such as depression or schizophrenia. Is substance abuse truly a mental disorder, or is it simply a chosen behavior—such as smoking (which also can be argued both ways)? Arguments can be made on both sides of this debate, but from the public policy perspective there is a more basic point to be made. Regardless of how responsible or irresponsible those struggling with substance use disorders may or may not have been at one point, it is clear that once addicted they need help. It is also obvious that to not provide help is to leave such a person in a state that is dangerous for self and costly for society. So from both an ethical and a pragmatic point of view, it makes good sense to offer effective substance abuse treatment along with other mental health services.

Substance abuse frequently co-occurs with serious mental illness, meaning that many who struggle with addictions also meet the criteria for a mental disorder and vice versa. These are sometimes referred to as "dual diagnosis" patients. Treatment is much more difficult if only part of a person's medical needs are covered by insurers. So for instance, currently a person struggling with both major depression and alcohol addiction may find that treatment is covered for depression but that any services for alcoholism must be paid for out of pocket. As a result, the depression is treated but not the accompanying addiction, making it likely that the patient will eventually relapse on both counts. Further, even when two relevant treatment programs are available, one for substance abuse and one for serious mental illness, they are often not coordinated or compatible. This means that the patient may receive care from two sources that is significantly mismatched (e.g., one calling for more independent living and the other calling for more group accountability). What is needed? A unified, transformed system of care consisting of evidence-based home and community services.

The substance that leads to addiction can be legal (e.g., alcohol), illegal (e.g., cocaine), or a prescription medication (e.g., painkillers). Once the person is addicted, a strong physiological component driving usage makes it almost impossible for the user to stop on his or her own. Epidemiological research shows that approximately 22.2 million people aged twelve and above are struggling with substance use disorders (SAMHSA 2006). One consequence of this is, of course, the illegal drug trade, which is driven by strong market demand and seems impervious to interdiction. Thus a side benefit to offering effective treatment for substance abuse is reduction in demand for illegal drugs.

Several treatment approaches are available for substance use disorders, including cognitive-behavioral therapy that deals with the automatic thoughts and underlying beliefs that drive addictive behavior. Different people respond well to different treatment programs, so it is important to have more than one type available if possible. At the same time, since many programs have not been demonstrated to be effective, it is easy to waste a good deal of time and money in search of help. The best-known treatment program is probably still the most effective for the largest numbers of those seeking help. Alcoholics Anonymous (with its related spin-offs such as Narcotics Anonymous) has been in existence since 1935 (Comer 2004). There are chapters in every major city, many hosted or run by churches or community organizations such as the Salvation Army. Research shows that faith-based organizations can be particularly effective with substance abuse treatment (Swora 2001, cited in Comer 2004).

However, the success rate of any treatment for substance use disorders is highly variable, with relapse as a frequent outcome. Here too there is a need for innovative treatment programs to be developed and tested. Furthermore, effective follow-up care in the home community is sorely lacking, which makes deterioration and relapse all the more likely.

Psychiatric Facility Care

Having glimpsed something of how difficult it is to manage a serious mental illness, the reader is now ready to appreciate how critical it is that effective and timely treatment be made available for all in need. This is nowhere more pressing than in psychiatric hospitals/facilities. Many of those confined there are committed against their will on the basis of judicial review that has found them to be mentally ill and a threat to self or others. This is one of the few cases in which a law-abiding citizen's basic right to freedom (to not be confined against one's will) is overruled by society. Once committed, an individual is completely at the mercy of those who staff the hospital. In some cases, the staff consists of warm-hearted, dedicated, and talented professionals who serve their patients tirelessly and make sure that time in the hospital is well spent. But in too many other cases, the committed patient is left in the care of those more focused on avoiding difficulties than treating patients. Such providers may be tempted to overmedicate psychiatric patients and turn on the TV to avoid the hassle of trying to improve life for someone with serious mental illness.

Unannounced Visits

I had only been commissioner of Virginia's Department of Mental Health, Mental Retardation, and Substance Abuse Services for about a year, but I had already become known as Commissioner "System Reform" Kelly, since my main message was that the mental health system was broken and in need of dramatic reforms. This was a welcome message to many of those receiving care, to many providers who knew we could do better, and to some of the department's administrators. But to many others, especially those comfortable with a status quo that provides good salary and benefits and doesn't ask too much in return, my message was anathema. For that reason, it was impossible to get an unbiased assessment of the quality of care in Virginia's psychiatric hospitals—called psychiatric "facilities." As with my first visit to the Lynchburg Training Center, whenever I officially planned and visited a facility I saw a carefully orchestrated show designed to say that all was well, and I knew it.

Virginia has sixteen psychiatric facilities originally built to house over fifteen thousand patients. Today there are fewer than three thousand hospitalized patients in Virginia, yet not one of the facilities has been closed. Why? Because each one is protected by a "patron saint" —its state legislator, who sees the facility as a critical source of jobs and votes in his or her district. Never mind that it takes more than $500 million a year to fund the facilities, or that those monies could be better spent on community services designed to help persons with serious mental illness succeed in their home community. My promotion, throughout my tenure, of the need to close one or more of Virginia's facilities and reinvest those funds in community mental health care did not endear me to the facility directors or their patron saints.[10]

Not surprisingly, I had found that unannounced visits were the only way to see what was really going on in the department's many psychiatric facilities. So at one point I found myself on the road, driving alone (to avoid tip-off) to drop in unannounced on a facility a few hours away from the Mental Health Department's central office in Richmond. I arrived late morning, went straight to the stunned director's office, declined his polite invitation to organize a staff meeting, and asked for an escort to get me onto the locked wards immediately—before news of my arrival spread. Sure enough, as I walked the halls of the locked units, this is what I found:

- The central assembly room was filled with staff and patients lounging together—sitting on couches or standing—and watching daytime TV.
- There was an overall "lazy" atmosphere—both staff and patients moving slowly and seemingly with little to do.
- Several patients were left alone in their rooms down the hall—unattended and seemingly overmedicated.
- A program of activities was posted on the wall, showing hour by hour what each patient was supposed to be doing (group therapy, art therapy, social skills training, etc.). But when I asked where these activities were taking place I found most had been cancelled for various reasons (staff not in that day, difficulties with patients, etc.).

Once again my suspicion had been confirmed. During a previous, official visit to this facility my staff and I had been proudly shown the list of program activities and had even (with patients' permission) sat in briefly on a group therapy session. Now I discovered to my dismay that programming was often the exception, not the rule—despite the daily posting of planned activities. The facility director "moved on" shortly thereafter, and the department's staff and I searched far and wide until we found a new person who specialized in hospital "turnarounds" to head up the facility. This got the attention of leadership throughout the Department of Mental Health and led to a new openness to innovation. Shortly thereafter, several of the facility directors collaborated to implement an innovative and newly developed concept—the "treatment mall."

A mental health treatment mall is designed to provide a selection of needed services and supports each day in a central place so that patients can go easily from area to area to find the treatment they need. This might involve training in social skills or hygiene, help in picking out new clothes and managing one's wardrobe, work with an anger management group, individual psychotherapy, or vocational training. Each morning the patients come to the treatment mall and are helped to select whatever is most appropriate for them, which varies depending on each person's progress. So for instance, a patient might end up working on social skills and hygiene and clothing, then on anger management, and then on vocational training before being discharged. The various programs are offered by staff trained in that area, with sensitivity to individualizing the training to meet each person's need. After the allotted block of time has been used, the patients move on to their next "appointment." Although this may require more staffing or new skills compared with custodial care, it is not inordinately expensive, since most staff can be easily retrained in these areas. The goal is for hospitalization to be marked by intensive and effective treatment, which also makes it more likely that the patient may be successfully discharged after a shorter-than-average stay. Thankfully, the average length of stay in psychiatric hospitals is decreasing and is now typically measured in days or weeks rather than months or years.

Treatment malls are not the solution to every facility problem, but they go a long way toward filling the void of use of time that is too often met with overmedication and TV. Nobody is left behind in his or her room, and nobody wastes the day away with television. Instead, everybody who is physically and emotionally capable joins in the treatment mall experience each day. In this way, daily programming is not just a theoretical list of activities on the wall. It is built into the facility's daily structure—both physical and programmatic. It should be noted that for hospitalization to succeed, planning for rehabilitation and recovery in the home community must begin long before discharge. There should be a smooth transition from brief hospitalization to intensive community care, which requires careful preparation and ongoing liaison with community services.

Persons with serious mental illness who are hospitalized against their will have the right to receive effective treatment, not just custodial care while medications are stabilizing, and to be returned to their home communities for effective follow-up care as soon as possible. Anything less is unethical, risky for the patient, unnecessarily burdensome on their family, and costly for the community that is deprived of a functioning citizen. It is time to transform America's broken system of mental health care.

Less Severe Mental Health Needs and Community Resources

Before proceeding, it is necessary to take a look at how less severe mental health needs should be met. If they are not to be included in the same category as serious mental illness, must they then be ignored altogether? Although the needs of individuals with serious mental illness should be met on a priority basis, those who suffer less severe needs must by no means be ignored. A compassionate society must assist all of those in need and should provide timely resources that can prevent less severe mental health problems from spiraling out of control. Without social support, for example, a person suffering bereavement is all the more vulnerable for a major depressive episode. Put another way, if a person's support network is not adequate, that could constitute the social component of the biopsychosocial model and thus trigger mental illness. Likewise, a person dealing with persistent sad feelings needs someone to offer support and a listening ear. Such imperatives are best understood as "mental health needs," and they can often be addressed by family, friends, church/synagogue/ mosque counselors, school counselors, employee assistance personnel, or social service nonprofit organizations. It would be a mistake for public and private insurers to conclude that all mental health matters must be addressed with the same urgency as serious mental illness, thereby reducing the prioritization of services for those with the greatest needs. Indigenous community resources can effectively address many mental health needs by offering the sensitive and personal care and support that they alone can provide. This allows insurers to focus all the more on addressing serious mental illness with well-funded, effective, innovative, community-based treatments.[11]

Community Resources

Needless to say, the most important community resource for dealing with mental health problems is one's own family and friends. A timely word of encouragement, practical help with a problem, and the support of loved ones who believe in us and walk with us through hard times are priceless resources for dealing with the storm and stress of life, and this support can help prevent the development of more serious mental health problems. In addition, other resources within the community can play a valuable role in preventing and addressing mental health needs.

- *Employers.* Large organizations often offer their workers Employee Assistance Programs (EAPs) that provide resources for managing stress, anxiety, anger, and grief. The EAP may provide gym privileges, yoga sessions, support groups, short-term counseling, or other sources of help. Access to these resources, for example, could help prevent an employee who is feeling overwhelmed with personal and professional stressors from experiencing a debilitating panic attack. Or they might help an employee work through the grief of a personal loss and thus avoid experiencing a major depression. Since serious mental illness is costly to both the employee and the employer, it is not only compassionate but also good fiscal policy for companies to provide effective EAPs.
- *Schools.* Schools can provide timely evaluation and appropriate support for children whose conduct is problematic, even while maintaining the importance of personal responsibility and parental involvement. Such support could be as simple as changing a child's classes to reduce academic or social frustration. Or it might involve working with the child's parents to explore opportunities for tutoring, mentoring, or sports activities. With parental approval, the child might also be referred to the school psychologist to provide counseling and guidance for dealing with stress, or perhaps to have

the child tested for attention deficit disorder or other emotional needs. It is important to deal with such needs as soon as possible, given that today's frustrated student could become tomorrow's dropout headed for even greater problems such as depression, substance abuse, or gang involvement.

- *Religious Institutions.* Churches, synagogues, and mosques can play a critical role in ministering to members who are struggling with mental health needs. Family members who are grieving over the loss of a loved one, older persons who are experiencing isolation and sadness, and couples having marital difficulties can all benefit from the support of their faith community. Many churches, for example, offer support groups and personal/pastoral counseling for those in need as well as twelve-step programs, which have proven to be very effective for many in dealing with addictions. Such support provides important resources for men and women of faith who are experiencing mental health needs and can help avert the development of major depression or other serious mental illnesses.[12]

- *Nonprofit Community Organizations.* Nonprofits such as the Boy Scouts and Girl Scouts, sports clubs, community centers, and other community-based organizations often play an important role in the lives of those who are faced with mental health needs. For instance, in scouting a boy or girl from a dysfunctional family may find the acceptance, camaraderie, and mentoring that is lacking at home. This support and sense of belonging can help protect youths from low self-esteem, depression, and self-destructive behaviors. It can also keep them from looking to gangs as a sort of surrogate family.

In these and other ways, resources within communities can help address the mental health needs of their residents and prevent them from spiraling into serious mental illness. Although individuals whose community offers few of these resources are at greater risk than those who have strong community support, the family or community must not be blamed for the emergence of serious mental illness. The biopsychosocial model makes it clear that mental illness is the result of a variety of factors—a "perfect storm" of contributing vulnerabilities and stressors. Thus it is far more appropriate to focus on providing effective resources for those who are suffering from mental health needs than it is to waste time and energy on pointing the finger of blame.

ation: The Road Map

The chapters that follow provide a road map for the transformation of America's mental health system of care. As noted earlier, five critical and interrelated topic areas are covered, since the new system of care must be

- *Results oriented:* Using results-oriented outcome measures and "evidence-based practices," which have been proven effective by empirical studies, so as to improve quality of care and system accountability.
- *Innovative:* Opening the monopolistic state mental health system to competition and innovation so as to improve effectiveness and increase treatment choices.
- *Adequately funded:* Implementing "parity" so that mental health treatment coverage matches physical health coverage.
- *Consumer friendly:* Empowering persons with serious mental illness—giving them and their families a real voice in policy development and service evaluation.
- *Committed to change:* Overcoming resistance to change from forces wed to the status quo.

A mental health system of care that is results oriented, innovative, consumer friendly, well funded, and committed to change cannot avoid transformation. These five key areas constitute a whole that, if implemented, will bring the service system into a time of dramatic and much-needed reform.

It is not surprising that various parties would like to move ahead in some but not all of these areas. Many mental health advocates support full parity between mental health and physical health coverage. But if this is accomplished without putting new evidence-based services in place, it will serve only to expand the status quo of ineffective care. Many insurers are calling for greater innovation and outcome-oriented accountability from providers but are not willing to pay the price for reform, including parity coverage and outcome data administrative costs. Many consumers are asking to be at the table for policy and treatment decisions, yet are hesitant to embrace outcome measures for fear these could be used to terminate treatment prematurely. For mental health reform to occur, it is clear that all parties must be willing to engage in the give-and-take of public discourse and negotiation. If one or more of these five key areas is not addressed because of resistance, there can be no comprehensive, enduring system transformation. Some brief changes may occur like a flash in the pan, as has happened many times on both state and federal levels. But genuine and lasting transformation requires sustained forward movement in all five areas, as will be shown in the following chapters.

2

That Which Is Measured Improves

Less than half of all mental health care is supported by *good* evidence. It will take decades to conduct comparative effectiveness studies, modify laws and change practitioner behavior.

> National Council for Community Behavioral
> Healthcare (2008)

That which is measured improves.

> Famous quote throughout leadership and management books, original author unknown

IT WAS THE summer of 1994, and I was just settling in as the newly appointed commissioner for Virginia's Department of Mental Health, Mental Retardation, and Substance Abuse Services. Monday morning at nine was our scheduled weekly staff meeting, when the commissioner and central office managers discuss strategic concerns and plan for the coming week. Like many, I was convinced that Virginia's mental health system was broken and in need of sweeping reforms and that it was time to get moving. As commissioner, and as a former academic, I wanted to begin the process of reform with a review of good, hard data. The department's budget was over half a billion dollars, and we had over ten thousand employees serving in fifteen state psychiatric facilities throughout Virginia. Additionally, there were forty county-based CMHCs whose programs were funded in part by our department. I wanted to know just what the result of this tremendous effort and activity was. My intention was to discuss who was served and how effective their services were, then to begin a top-to-bottom review of Virginia's programs and services as a first step toward needed reforms.

I turned to the director of the Office of Management Information Systems and asked a question that I assumed was quite simple: "Tell me, how many people do we serve on a yearly basis, both in the psychiatric facilities and throughout the community mental health centers?"

Awkward silence, a clearing of the throat, then a somewhat sheepish "We have no way of determining that."

"Excuse me?"

"We do not track how many people we treat, or even basic demographics such as age and gender. We only tabulate the units of service delivered, which must be regularly reported to our funding sources.[1] Since many of our clients receive multiple services over the course of a year, units of service data include duplicated counts and so cannot tell us how many people are served." I was stunned, and from that point forward spent a great deal of time and effort uncovering what came to seem like an episode from the Theater of the Absurd. This vast, multi-hundred-million-dollar state agency couldn't even count its customers—much less determine to what extent they were helped.

I came to find out that most other states were in the same boat. In 1995, I was elected to serve on the board of directors of the National Association of State Mental Health Program Directors, the national organization that represents state mental health agencies. As such, I was privy to confidential information that confirmed my worst fears. With just a few exceptions, it was no better in other states. Several factors contribute to this unfortunate state of affairs, including that in many cases mental health services are assigned a low priority among pressing state needs. For one thing, there is not much of an organized voting constituency in the ranks of persons with serious mental illness.

But another factor is often overlooked. State agencies such as departments of mental health are by definition monopolies and often lack a private-sector managerial mind-set. There is no competition and therefore no real impetus to improve efficiency, to improve quality of care, or to ensure that the customers, or "consumers," of state mental health services are satisfied with the services they receive.

As a monopoly, the agency has no particular requirement for the kind of information a competitive private-sector organization would demand, such as who is receiving which services and the level of customer satisfaction. All that is usually required for funding to continue, whether from state or federal sources, is to report the units of service delivered on a regular basis and make the case that more is needed. So it makes perfect sense that the information tallied by Virginia's Department of Mental Health was just that—the units of service delivered. Unfortunately, this is too often the case even today. Although many states have attempted to move their mental health agencies toward outcome-oriented data, it has proven to be a difficult process that is slow in coming.

What is the solution to this lack of critical management information? It is to measure the actual outcome of clinical care in the lives of those receiving services and make those data (aggregated with no identifying information) available to mental health policy makers, providers, consumers, and third-party payers (public- and private-sector insurers). Managers have long noted that that which is measured improves, since no one wants to turn in a poor report card (e.g., Drucker 2003). Accordingly, measuring clinical outcomes tends to improve results by focusing on just how well those receiving care are doing. If such information were readily available on a routine basis, it would by definition make clear what is working well in the lives of consumers and what isn't. By so doing, this would shed light on those areas of the mental health service system that are sorely in need of reform, or transformation. As commissioner, I was fond of saying that providing mental health care without the benefit of outcome data was like trying to perform surgery in a darkened room. It's difficult to tell exactly what's going on or how to make sure the patient comes out okay. Using clinical outcome measures is like turning on a light in the room. Suddenly it's much clearer what's working well, what isn't, and what needs to be done to improve results for those struggling with serious mental illness so that they can have a life of recovery in their home community. This chapter is about how to turn that light on.

Clinical Outcome Data

Just what is meant by clinical outcome data? When you are ill and visit your doctor, he or she typically asks you to describe in some detail how you're doing physically. You may say that your throat hurts, you're congested, you're running a high fever, and consequently you've had to stay home from work. The doctor examines you to confirm the symptoms, concludes that you have a bad cold, and prescribes treatment such as medication and rest. You are asked to report back a few days later. Assuming you get better, you report that your throat is fine, you are no longer congested, the fever is gone, and you're able to return to work. That constitutes clinical outcome data in the arena of physical health, in this case involving the remediation of three symptoms (sore throat, congestion, fever) and a return to normal functioning in the workplace.

The status of a person's mental health is of course more difficult to determine than that of his or her physical health. A person suffering from depression, bipolar disorder, or even schizophrenia looks no different from anyone else and has no physical symptoms such as a fever or cough that can be examined. A mental health provider asks the patient to describe in some detail how he or she is doing emotionally but must rely on self-report rather than a physical exam. If a consumer states that for some time he has cried daily and does not want to get out of bed, cannot eat or sleep well, has no energy, has thoughts of hurting himself, and has been unable to go to work, the likely conclusion is that he is suffering from depression and would benefit from psychotherapy and possibly antidepressant medication. The consumer checks in regularly over the course of several months for psychotherapy, medication monitoring, or both and at some point will be asked to report how it's going. Assuming improvement, the consumer reports that he is no longer overcome with grief or plagued with thoughts of self-harm, is able to eat and sleep well, has plenty of energy, and is effectively going about his daily business. That constitutes mental health clinical outcome data, in this case involving the remediation of five symptoms of depression (sadness, suicidal thoughts, poor eating and sleeping, low energy) and a return to normal functioning (being able to go to work).

But here is the problem. Whereas with a physical illness the doctor can verify the presence or absence of disease using a standardized, objective physical examination, the mental health provider is essentially limited to the consumer's self-report. The specific symptoms of all mental illnesses are listed in the *Diagnostic and Statistical Manual of Mental Disorders* (American Psychiatric Association 2000), and can be checked off for diagnostic purposes, but these (with a few exceptions) are not open to physical examination. This means that the diagnostic and treatment process is inherently more subjective for mental health care than for medical/surgical care. It also means that it is difficult to determine just how well the recipient of mental health care is doing at any given time. If after six weeks of treatment a person with depression says he is not doing much better, does that mean treatment is not working? Who is to decide? Even worse, suppose the consumer and provider disagree on whether there has been improvement? Which one is correct? A Vanderbilt University study looked at clinical outcomes for consumers being treated for depression from three perspectives: that of the provider, that of the consumer, and that of an objective observer. The consumers and observers both reported that about 83 percent of those in care improved—not a bad rate of success. However, the providers reported that 100 percent of their patients improved, thus suggesting that a positive bias may at times influence providers' outcome assessments (Kelly and Strupp 1992, 37). This does not mean that the provider's assessment of outcome is not important; it is. But it does mean that clinical outcome data should always include the consumer's perspective as well.

Clinical Outcome Research

The question of clinical effectiveness has been the focus of much research and publication—especially over the last twenty-five years. Clinical outcome research has clearly demonstrated the effectiveness of cognitive and interpersonal therapy and antidepressant medications for treating depression, the effectiveness of cognitive and systematic desensitization therapy and antianxiety medication for treating anxiety disorders, and the importance of the therapeutic relationship (Bickman 2005; Seligman 1994; Shadish et al. 2000).[2] Since this research requires the use of clinical surveys, there is a growing body of literature on standardized clinical outcome measures and their uses. There is also growing research-based literature on big-picture questions such as how effective therapy is, overall, for treating mental illness. For instance, "meta-analytic" outcome studies have been very helpful for informing public- and private-sector policy makers' discussions on which treatments should or should not be covered by insurers (Office of Technology Assessment 1994; Smith, Glass, and Miller 1980).[3]

Martin Seligman demonstrated in the mid-1990s what has since become widely accepted: that a survey of those receiving care in the field is in fact the "gold standard" of data for establishing clinical effectiveness. Also, he pointed to the two primary focuses a clinical outcome survey must cover: symptom reduction and functional life improvement (Seligman 1995).

Drawing on this growing body of clinical effectiveness literature, several teams of researchers have developed core outcome batteries of questionnaires that meet the needs of researchers, clinicians, consumers, insurers, and policy makers alike (e.g., Barkham et al. 1998; Borkovec et al.

2001). However, despite the availability of these scientifically proven and clinically useful outcome measures, many researchers "are struck by how slow the field has been to deal adequately with the subtleties of outcome measurement" (Jacobson et al. 1999, 306). There is strong resistance from some quarters, as will be discussed below.

Outcome-Oriented Practice

What is needed is for the field to adopt a scientifically credible and con-sumer-focused methodology with which mental health providers can as-sess and document their patients' clinical improvements. It must be based on the consumer's self-report, since that is the most direct source of in-formation,[4] and it must be scientifically sound—objective, standardized, and uniformly applied. By *objective* we mean that the outcome data would be interpreted the same way by any mental health provider and is thus not based on subjective interpretation. For example, assuming honest re-sponses, it is clear that a consumer who scored very high on a depression scale at intake (e.g., the Beck Depression Inventory) and now at termina-tion is in the normal range has improved.[5] By *standardized* we mean that the questionnaire has been tested with many populations so that normal and abnormal ranges of responses have been scientifically established. Thus there is confidence that a consumer who initially scored in the ab-normal range for depression but after treatment scores solidly in the nor-mal range has indeed improved. *Uniformly applied* means that the same measures are being used by other mental health providers (to the extent possible) so that results can be validly compared.

Thankfully, over the past twenty years, standardized, objective clinical outcome measures have been developed and tested for use with just about every population and treatment setting (child/adult, inpatient/outpatient/ community based, etc.) and for just about any diagnosis (e.g., Corcoran and Fischer 2000). These measures are basically questionnaires, or mea-suring "instruments," designed to be minimally burdensome on those who fill them out, yet comprehensive enough to capture improvement in the most relevant areas. The questions, or "items," used on these instruments have been honed through research to be clear and concise and to capture areas where improvements have been made as well as areas where further needs must be addressed. For example, an item might read: "During the past week I have felt down or depressed: a) all the time, b) frequently, c) daily, d) occasionally, e) never." Assuming careful and honest responses, items like this yield important information that, when taken together, produce an accurate profile of the consumer's mental health status.

Before being marketed, these instruments are put through rigorous tests to ensure that they are both reliable and valid. By *reliable* we mean that the instrument's results are stable. For instance, if a respondent completes a depression questionnaire on Monday and again on Tuesday, the results should be the same (assuming no improvement). By *valid* we mean that the items address the desired target and only that. Questions must be phrased in such a way that the respondent clearly understands what is being asked. For instance, it would not be appropriate to ask, "Have you recently felt down or angry?" since it would be impossible to tell by the response which feeling was being endorsed.

There are currently many reliable and valid standardized mental health outcome measures available, such as the Treatment Outcome Package and the CORE Outcome Measure, both developed for use in outpatient mental health clinics.[6] These are sometimes referred to as "core batteries" or "core measures." Typically, they contain around thirty-five to forty questions and take about twenty minutes to complete. The categories they address are the same covered in your doctor's office—symptoms (symptomatology) and level of functioning (functionality). Their items must cover the range of symptoms normally seen with a given population and setting, as well as how well one is functioning at home, at work, or at school. Following is a sample of items typically found in such measures, which usually must be answered on a five-point scale ranging from "all the time" to "never":

Symptomatology:
- I have trouble making decisions.
- I feel tired and have little energy.
- I think about killing myself.
- I have little or no appetite.
- I am worried about going crazy.
- I have unwanted thoughts or images.
- I have seen or heard something that was not really there.

Functionality:
- My work performance has been criticized.
- I have missed school or work.
- I am in conflict with those close to me.

Although symptomatology and functionality are usually sufficient for applied clinical outcome measurement, one other category is often included as well—the consumer's overall sense of satisfaction with services received. Satisfaction with services is of course a goal for mental health consumers, just as it would be with customers of any service, and should be fairly high from day one of treatment.

The above sample items would typically be appropriate in outpatient settings but could also be used in inpatient settings such as a psychiatric hospital. However, inpatient settings also need to address other concerns that go beyond symptom reduction, functional improvement, and service satisfaction. For instance, use of seclusion and restraints, reliance on medications, adequacy of discharge planning, and readmission rates would all be appropriate additional outcome measures with which to evaluate quality of care in inpatient settings.

How often outcome measures are used depends upon the consumer's needs, the setting, and other factors. For instance, in an intense inpatient setting such as a psychiatric hospital acute ward, symptoms may need to be checked daily. In a typical outpatient setting where the consumer is coming for weekly services, once every four weeks may be sufficient. In every setting the goal is to measure frequently enough to capture important changes early on, yet infrequently enough so as not to unnecessarily burden the consumer or the provider.

In sum, scientifically sound and easy-to-use clinical outcome measures are readily available for just about any mental health service setting. Unfortunately, they are not yet widely used as a matter of course by either public-sector or private-sector providers. There is currently little fiscal incentive to do so, but that may be changing. Public and private insurers are just beginning to require clinical outcome data for continued funding. Consequently, a small but growing number of both mental health agencies and private organizations are experimenting with outcome measures. They are spurred on by the call for results-oriented mental health reforms and the related call for using only "evidence-based practices."

Evidence-Based Practice

The history of mental health care is strewn with practices that now make one cringe when reading about them. Locking persons with serious mental illness away in closets or warehousing them without treatment in run-down "lunatic asylums," overmedicating them to keep them under control in a zombielike state, performing lobotomies on them (as portrayed in the movie *One Flew Over the Cuckoo's Nest*)—all these practices were commonly accepted at one time. If the consumer or family members ever questioned the wisdom of such actions, they were assured by the authorities that they were appropriate. Until the 1970s, the question of the appropriateness and effectiveness of mental health treatment was seldom raised and, if ever it was, was simply left up to the treating authorities in charge. If the authorities decided a certain treatment was in order, it was carried out without question.

But since that time there has been a steady and much-needed march toward the promotion of evidence-based practice. In the late 1970s, for example, an outcome-oriented research-based treatment approach was developed for persons who were chronically mentally ill, called Assertive Community Treatment (ACT; Dixon and Goldman 2003). This involved sending mental health professionals into the community to provide whatever was needed for the patient to succeed—at home, at school, or at work. The treatment proved to be very effective in reducing the percentage of those who cycled from psychiatric hospitals to the streets and back again, and it is frequently referred to as a model evidence-based practice.

In 1980, the American Psychiatric Association published a new version of the *Diagnostic and Statistical Manual of Mental Disorders* (third edition) using research-based diagnostic criteria (American Psychiatric Association 1980). These criteria, which consist of the symptoms of mental disorders, gave newfound specificity to the definition and diagnosis of mental illnesses. Such specificity allowed for the growth of outcome-oriented research that focused on symptom reduction, usually targeting the point at which the consumer became symptom free. By studying a service's ability to effectively reduce symptomatology, researchers are identifying evidence-based treatments. In other words, the "evidence" of evidence-based practice is that of symptom reduction.

Throughout the 1980s and 1990s, a growing number of researchers and policy makers began calling for evidence-based practices, especially in the United Kingdom. The Cochrane Collaboration, based in Oxford since 1993, is dedicated to the promotion of evidence-based practices and maintains a library of current relevant research (e.g., Clarke and Oxman 1999; see www.cochrane.org). A British journal titled *Evidence-Based Mental Health* is also dedicated to the topic and to helping mental health providers stay abreast of the latest practice-relevant evidence (see ebmh.

bmjjournals.com). Thankfully, British empiricism is alive and well in the form of evidence-based mental health practice.

Over the last ten years, a growing body of research literature has succeeded in establishing the definition, importance, and practical usefulness of evidence-based mental health practices (e.g., Clarke and Oxman 1999; Corrigan, McCracken, and McNeilly 2005; Davies, Nutley, and Smith 2000; Dixon and Goldman 2003; Drake, Merrens, and Lynde 2005; Glicken 2004; Hillman 2002; Kelly 2003a, 2003b; Lambert, Hansen, and Finch 2001; Merrens 2005; Nathan and Gorman 2002; Roth and Fonagy 1996). As a result, an increasing number of policy makers and insurers are expecting that treatments or services offered for a person with mental illness will first be subjected to scientific outcome-oriented testing and found to be effective. It is important to note that the testing involved for establishing evidence-based practices requires using clinical outcome data. In fact, they can be seen as two sides of one coin. It is not possible to determine which treatments are effective without referring to clinical outcome data, and the natural result of such data as they accumulate is to identify evidence-based practices—treatments that work well.

In the mid-1990s, for example, the National Institute of Mental Health funded a large clinical trial comparing the effectiveness of interpersonal psychotherapy, cognitive-behavioral psychotherapy, and SSRI antidepressants in treating depression. The researchers found that all three were effective in treating major depression (Elkin 1994). Subsequently, the field has identified a growing array of evidence-based practices for treating depression and other disorders that includes interpersonal psychotherapy, cognitive-behavioral therapy, and SSRI antidepressants. Since these treatments have a growing body of clinical outcome research demonstrating their effectiveness, providers have confidence that their use will indeed help those in need.

The hope is that all mental health treatments will eventually be evidence based and that those that are ineffective will be weeded out. It is likely that in the not-too-distant-future mental health insurers will require that all covered services consist of evidence-based practices. But that has not yet happened, and consequently many mental health providers continue to offer services that cannot claim to be evidence based, with questionable results. In fact, one study found that less than 15 percent of consumers currently receive evidence-based mental health services (Merrens 2005). Evidence-based practices are too often rejected by providers who favor traditional therapeutic approaches, especially if they have been trained in old practices rather than newer ones that have been tested for effectiveness. It is as if the field of mental health services suspects that evidence-based practice may well be the hallmark of future care but cannot bring itself to let go of old ways. We are addicted to the status quo!

Furthermore, it is possible to support the general need for providers to use evidence-based practices even while rejecting the use of real-time case-by-case clinical outcome data to guide care for individual patients. In other words, some policy makers are comfortable with requiring evidence-based treatments but not with having consumers use outcome surveys on a regular basis, even though it was those surveys that identified the evidence-based treatments in the first place. Outcome surveys are seen as too burdensome, too threatening, too expensive, or simply unnecessary. This is unfortunate, as it deprives the consumer of determining to what extent he or she is truly benefiting from a particular treatment at a particular time. After all, even if a treatment is evidence based, that does not prove that it is the best selection for a given person with his or her particular array of needs and vulnerabilities. The only objective way to determine that is to use standardized clinical outcome measures on an individual, real-time basis to ensure that treatment is having its intended effect.

Clinical Outcomes in Virginia: The Performance Outcomes Measurement System

In Virginia in the mid-1990s, an outcome-oriented pilot project was developed called the Performance Outcomes Measurement System pilot project (POMS), designed to introduce clinical outcome measures to the state's many mental health providers (Blank, Koch, and Burkett 2004; Kelly 1997).[7] The hope was that this would help spark systemwide mental health reform by providing data showing what worked well and what didn't.

POMS employed several standardized instruments that could be used in inpatient settings, in outpatient settings, and with different populations (adults with serious mental illness, children and adolescents with serious emotional disturbances, and persons dealing with substance abuse). The instruments were chosen to be clinically useful for the provider while also being able to generate ongoing programmatic outcome data. This was a first for the state of Virginia, if not most states, and it required a great deal of give-and-take by all parties to overcome initial skepticism. For instance, there was concern that the state's providers did not have adequate information technology resources required for such a project. So we at the Department of Mental Health agreed to supply the hardware, software, and training needed to manage clinical outcome data. Once the pilot was up and running, its benefits were notable. The data output helped providers with case management and also helped program managers to identify which programs and services were most effective for which consumers.

National Clinical Outcomes:
SAMHSA's National Outcome Measures

Virginia was one of the first states whose mental health agency developed and implemented clinical outcome measures, as illustrated by the POMS initiative. Since that time several other states have begun moving in that direction, as has the primary federal agency that funds mental health services, the Substance Abuse and Mental Health Services Administration (SAMHSA). SAMHSA has begun developing potential national outcome measures for mental health services (NOMs), drawing on experiences in Virginia and elsewhere, that include measures of symptomatology, functionality, and consumer satisfaction. NOMs also include other important service considerations such as use of hospitalization, use of evidence-based practices, and overall program cost-effectiveness. SAMHSA is encouraging state mental health agencies to begin using these measures on an elective basis. Following is a selection from the NOMs list of key outcomes:

- Decreased symptomatology
- Improved functionality at work or school
- Improved stability/functionality at home
- Client perception of care
- Abstinence from drug and alcohol abuse (if applicable)
- Decreased criminal justice involvement (if applicable)
- Reduced usage of psychiatric inpatient beds (if applicable)
- Use of evidence-based practices
- Cost-effectiveness

This is clearly a step in the right direction, as it is the first time the federal government has successfully promoted a credible set of standardized clinical outcome measures for nationwide use. It is in fact a long-overdue action that many mental health researchers and advocates have been calling for for years (Barkham et al. 1998, 2001; Corrigan, McCracken, and McNeilly 2005; Drake, Merrens, and Lynde 2005; Evans et al. 2000; Grob and Goldman 2006; Kelly 1997, 2000, 2002a, 2002b, 2003a, 2003b; Kraus, Seligman, and Jordan 2005; Manderscheid 1998, 1999; Mental Health Statistics Improvement Program [MHSIP] Task Force 1996; National Association of State Mental Health Program Directors [NASMHPD] Research Institute 1998; President's New Freedom Commission on Mental Health 2003; Office of the Surgeon General 1999). SAMHSA's hope is for states to begin voluntarily using NOMs on a regular basis, thus generating detailed and comparative clinical outcome data that will help promote system improvements. Of course, not everyone is happy with this prospect, as will be discussed below, and it is an open question whether state mental health agencies will implement the use of NOMs on a regular basis.

If the states implement these measures uniformly, the "light" will be turned on and providers, policy makers, insurers, and consumers alike will be able to see clearly what works well and for whom. By the same token, if an innovative private-sector company implements standardized clinical outcome measures and reaps the benefits of improved efficiency and quality of care, others will no doubt follow suit. It only takes a spark to get this fire going, and that spark could come from leadership within either the public or private sector, as we will see in chapter 6 when we discuss leadership.

The New Freedom Commission on Mental Health

In 2000, presidential candidate George W. Bush began talking about how to better care for persons with disabilities, including those with mental illness. This discussion was presented as a follow-up to the Americans with Disabilities Act (ADA) that his father had passed as president in 1990.[8] George W. Bush stated that he intended to expand the scope of the ADA by addressing the needs of persons with serious mental illness, among other disabilities. It had been a quarter-century since the last national mental health commission during the Carter administration (see Foley and Sharfstein 1983), and many agreed that the field was ripe for reform. Consequently, a campaign promise was made to launch a federal mental health commission to evaluate the field of mental health care and make recommendations for reform. Upon election, this led to the creation of a presidential commission called the New Freedom Commission on Mental Health.

The commission invited testimony from many concerned with the need for mental health reform, including myself. My testimony encouraged the members to focus on the critical role of clinical outcome measurement (Kelly 2002a). The commission produced a final report with some timely recommendations, including the following six goals:

1. Americans understand that mental health is essential to overall health.
2. Mental health care is consumer and family driven.
3. Disparities in mental health services are eliminated.
4. Early mental health screening, assessment, and referral to services are common practice.
5. Excellent mental health care is delivered and research is accelerated.
6. Technology is used to access mental health care and information.

The commission gave a much-needed boost to the call for mental health transformation by drawing attention to the brokenness of the current system of care and by focusing on recovery as an appropriate treatment outcome. It stated that "America's mental health service delivery system is in shambles" (President's New Freedom Commission on Mental Health 2002, i) . . . [and] . . . "presents barriers that all too often add to the burden of mental illnesses for individuals, their families, and our communities. . . . The Commission recommends a fundamental transformation of the nation's approach to mental health care. This transformation must ensure that mental health services and supports actively facilitate recovery" (President's New Freedom Commission on Mental Health 2003, 1).

Thus the commission gave presidential authority to the claim that the current mental health system is indeed broken and desperately in need of transformation. Furthermore, the report specified consumer recovery as the appropriate goal for effective care. This is meant to suggest, not that persons with serious mental illness can be cured, but that they can be helped to return successfully to their home community—to have a real home, a fulfilling job, and deep relationships. Recovery means successfully integrating a mental disorder into a consumer's overall lifestyle—enabling him or her to craft a full, productive life and thereby to minimize dependence on the service system. Recovery-oriented care thus provides a win-

win scenario both ethically and economically. Not only is it the right thing to do on behalf of persons who must otherwise live their lives on the margins of society, but it also enables them to be economically productive members of the home community.

But how are we to measure progress toward excellent mental health care and the ultimate goal of recovery? How will we know when and whether we get there unless we begin to use standardized, objective, uniformly applied clinical outcome measures? Unfortunately the commission stopped short of explicitly recommending measures such as NOMs, though it did lay the groundwork for moving in that direction. Perhaps this is because the commission was charged by the Bush administration to develop recommendations that would be minimally costly, and implementation of national outcome measures would indeed require significant funding. Yet unless requisite funding is provided for outcome measures, unless the "light" of outcome data is turned on, the mental health system transformation called for in the report cannot succeed.

SAMHSA has been charged with leading the national effort toward implementation of the commission's findings. Consequently, it has refocused many of its activities and programs around the six commission goals as listed above and their related objectives. This means SAMHSA is attempting to guide the states' mental health agencies toward implementation of commission goals via grant opportunities, primarily the Mental Health Transformation State Incentive Grants. These grants are designed to help the states begin the process of transforming their mental health service delivery system in a comprehensive manner, with all the stakeholders at the table. It is a step in the right direction in that it gets everyone talking about what a new mental health system might look like. But unless all five areas covered in this book are addressed, efforts will stall and any lasting changes will fall far short of what is needed for genuine system transformation.

In sum, the commission clearly identified major problems in the mental health service system and pointed toward potential solutions, if somewhat timidly. Now it is up to others to take up the challenge and move forward. It takes courage and innovation from the public and private sectors to tackle those problems and to lead the way with outcome-oriented solutions. Both sectors have a lot to gain in terms of rooting out waste, promoting quality of care, and ending up with truly satisfied consumers of mental health services.

What's Wrong with Clinical Outcome Data?

If the collection of clinical outcome data is so important, why isn't everyone calling for it? What could possibly be wrong with measuring the extent to which a person has been helped by mental health care? The answer depends on who you are, since providers, insurers, and consumers have very different concerns regarding this matter.

Providers

Many mental health providers see the value of clinical outcome data as a way to help them do their best with each consumer and are willing to take reasonable steps in that direction. But others feel that outcome measures constitute simply one more intrusion in the consumer-provider relationship, as well as an unpaid administrative drain on already-stretched time. They are simply not willing to administer, score, and track patient results unless and until third-party payers cover the time and effort required. Consequently, some researchers are pessimistic about how quickly the field will actually adopt outcome measures, since adoption would require a "major change in clinical practice patterns." Routinely measuring outcomes, according to some, "is not likely to become a practice standard in the foreseeable future" (Lambert, Hansen, and Finch 2001, 169).

Additionally, there is concern that the resultant data could be used punitively by reviewers who may not take into account differences among consumer populations. For instance, although significant functional improvement at work, school, or home is the expected outcome for most patients, that is not the case for all consumers. For those with the most severe cases of mental illness (e.g., chronic paranoid schizophrenia), simple maintenance of current functioning may be an appropriate expected outcome. If these differences in consumer populations are not taken into account, then outcome data may make providers who work with the most severe cases of mental illness appear ineffective in contrast with other providers. Clearly, the solution is for population and situational differences always to be carefully taken into account when analyzing outcome data.

Further, most mental health providers are very familiar with managed care procedures and utilization review, in which application is made to insurance reviewers to authorize coverage for continued treatment. Consequently, some providers fear that outcome measures may simply be used to add to the complexity and burden of utilization review.

It is certainly understandable that some providers may fear that clinical outcome data will be misused or that punitive (rather than remedial) actions will be taken if their patients do not improve. It is also understandable that some providers cringe at the idea of an additional unpaid administrative requirement. Both of these concerns must be addressed. Indeed, it is critical that as outcome measures become required the resultant data are used to support the good-faith clinical efforts of the mental health provider. If outcomes are not as expected, then remediation or referral, not punishment, is in order. If outcomes are consistently below expectations for a given provider or program, then perhaps further training would be in order. If further training is not successful, then and only then should consideration be given to shifting funds to a more effective program or provider.

It is also critical that the providers' administrative burden in managing the flow of outcome data be adequately reimbursed. If policy makers or insurers want to require the use of outcome measures, then they must realistically cover the cost of time and effort, without reducing pay for services. In other words, new funds will be required (e.g., from increases in insurance premiums). Otherwise compliance will be sporadic and begrudging at best. Thankfully these concerns are not insoluble. They can and must be resolved fairly, with give-and-take from both sides. It is surprising how collaborative and flexible opposing parties can be when they both have fiscal incentive to do so (providers improve care and demand for services; insurers get better results for their money).

The use of outcome measures comes easier to providers who are comfortable with a more behavioral approach to treatment such as cognitive-behavioral therapy (see Meichenbaum 1977). Over the past two decades, cognitive-behavioral therapy has become the most widely endorsed psychotherapeutic approach both among mental health providers and among faculty at university-based doctoral psychology training programs (Prochaska and Norcross 2003). There are many reasons for this, including the fact that cognitive-behavioral therapy tends to be problem focused, outcome oriented, defined as an evidence-based practice, and shorter term than other modalities such as psychodynamic psychotherapy. Because cognitive-behavioral therapy is an evidence-based practice that recommends using real-time outcome measures, its adherents are by definition more at ease using clinical outcome data.

Psychodynamically oriented providers tend to focus more on personal history and relationships, including the therapeutic relationship between the provider and the patient. Some feel that outcome measures disrupt that relationship by putting the provider in the role of evaluator/ enforcer of improvement. While this may sometimes be the case if it is not carefully managed, outcome data need not trouble the therapeutic relationship any more than simply asking the consumer how she is faring. With few exceptions, everyone suffering from serious mental illness wants to get better, and outcome data provide a structured way to address the topic of improvement and bring it into the therapy session for discussion. It can then be processed within the context of the therapeutic relationship as more grist for the mill.

I have found that most consumers appreciate any efforts to ensure their improvement, including the use of clinical measures. In fact, I found that the use of clinical outcome measures can actually be appreciated by all parties. As a licensed psychologist working in the D.C. area, I participated in an outpatient practice that was experimenting with the implementation of outcome measures in the early 1990s. We found that our consumers (lower- to middle-class adults dealing with mood or anxiety disorders or managing schizophrenia) generally appreciated the extra "positive outcome effort" made on their behalf, especially when results were used to inform therapy. We also found that insurers appreciated requests for continued care authorization accompanied by standardized data showing which major symptoms remained. Most often, reauthorization was granted. Further, the clinicians appreciated having regular objective feedback on how well each patient was doing. Properly used, outcome data can help both the provider and the insurer to work effectively and compassionately toward symptom remediation and improved life functioning on a case-by-case basis.

Insurers

Third-party payers are very interested in the possibility of clinical outcome data improving the quality of funded care, as well as the opportunity to build results-oriented accountability into mental health services. Already some insurance companies and governmental agencies are requesting that providers use evidence-based practices whenever possible. The use of clinical outcome measures takes that one step further by making sure that the treatment offered not only is statistically proven but works well for each individual consumer. Third-party payers have a lot to gain by using outcome data. But at the same time some insurers note that the collecting of information is not without cost and that the resultant data could be used to justify additional care beyond usual provisions. In other words, there is concern about having to pay for the cost of surveying as well as for additional services if the survey data show further need. Furthermore, there is concern that outcome instruments could yield inaccurate measures of the consumer's actual clinical needs or could perhaps be gamed by either consumers or providers to indicate need for services ad infinitum.

Given the strong psychometric properties of state-of-the-art clinical outcome measures, which means that their results are reliable and valid, accuracy is not a concern so long as the questions are carefully and honestly answered. The items have been honed through painstaking research so that they yield an accurate view of the respondent's actual clinical status. Consumers, providers, and insurers alike are usually pleasantly surprised at the extent to which clinical surveys provide accurate and revealing profiles of the patient's needs. For example, I have had patients who were relieved to acknowledge what a depression survey revealed—that they were still significantly depressed despite denying it to themselves and others.

At the same time, the potential for inaccuracies should be addressed. It is possible to imbed a "fake-bad scale" of improbable answers in the survey to detect those who may be trying to game the system (as is done with the Minnesota Multiphasic Personality Inventory [MMPI], a popular measure of psychopathology). This is a group of questions that are designed to be sensitive to someone who is exaggerating difficulties. If the respondent is either unable or unwilling to provide careful, honest answers, then the results are invalid and will be so indicated on the survey. Further, a consumer who has difficulty with the reading level required or with the language (although most measures are available in multiple languages) may unintentionally provide inaccurate data. But this can usually be detected by the random nature of responses and can be corrected by having someone verbally walk through the items with the consumer.

If the respondent is unwilling to provide honest and accurate information for any reason (e.g., not wanting to terminate care even though all treatment goals are met), this will become clear by the pattern of data and by the fake-bad scale (if used). Thus it is possible to detect those who may try to game the system by carefully analyzing the survey data and noting the improvement trajectory. For instance, if a person initially struggling with major depression has actually improved but tries to fake-bad in order to continue receiving services, he or she will typically generate a profile showing satisfaction with current services yet a lack of improvement. This serves as a red flag, since consumers who are not getting better are usually (and understandably) dissatisfied with their current services. In such a case, the provider could be asked to resolve the discrepancy by carefully reviewing the consumer's clinical status. (As an additional administrative burden, the time required must be covered by the third-party payer.) Given the sophistication of software programs that are used to score and interpret clinical outcome measures, it is not difficult to screen for patterns of data that indicate possibly invalid questionnaires, which can then be double-checked.

Insurers should welcome the use of outcome measures, since it seems clear that benefits would outweigh costs. Costs include the fact that insurers must fund the administrative component and must authorize additional services when these are indicated by the outcome data. Benefits include confidence that the consumer (and insurer) are getting what they are paying for—effective care. Surely it is better for insurers to know that funded services are effective, even if it costs something to find that out, than to continue to pour money into ineffective treatments. Further, it is inevitable that outcome data will lead to improvement in the overall efficiency and effectiveness of covered services, since what is working or not comes to light, thus improving quality of care for the most reasonable cost. If some cases may require additional care based on the outcome data, that is likely to be offset by other cases that will be appropriate for termination once the data show that clinical needs have been well met.

Additionally, insurers who are willing to lead in this area will reap the benefit of becoming known for quality of care in mental health services. The innovation and commonsense appeal of outcome-oriented care may be marketed to great advantage over competitors who continue with business as usual, devoid of performance data.

Consumers

I have found that most consumers of mental health services like the idea of their improvement being monitored, taken seriously, and based on their own feedback. After all, it means that their assessment of treatment will be helping to shape their own care. This is the ultimate consumer-oriented and individualized treatment approach, since the outcome data used for case management are actually the voice of the one receiving care. Nonetheless, some consumers worry that filling out the surveys could be burdensome, that information may not be kept confidential, or that the results could be used to prematurely terminate care (once they show improvement). These are understandable concerns, but they can all be resolved fairly easily.

Regarding the question of burden, it is critical that outcome measures be selected that take no more than twenty minutes to complete. This is a short enough time not to disrupt schedules and may simply mean that the consumer comes in a little early, say, every fourth session. This author found that the vast majority of consumers in an outpatient setting in the Washington, D.C., area willingly came early and completed their outcome measures, convinced that it meant they would receive better care. Indeed, this was the case, as the outcome data often helped the provider fine-tune therapy. Persons with serious mental illness in inpatient settings are likely to require more time, and perhaps some help, to complete the surveys. But this is time well spent, even if staff efforts are required.

Regarding confidentiality, it is of course imperative that all clinical outcome data be kept absolutely confidential and that only aggregated data (which consist of averages and include no identifying information) be used for program review. Individual data must be used only to authorize further care and must always remain strictly confidential. As for using data to prematurely terminate care, this must be addressed in the same manner as any issue regarding coverage. It is up to the insurer to make clear just what will or will not be covered in various scenarios and for various costs. Significant reduction of the consumer's symptoms and return to a normal level of functioning provide a reasonable target for treatment termination, but the precise definition of both must be made clear to consumers and policy makers up front. On-paper-only improvement is not acceptable—only real recovery. Also, appeals mechanisms and emergency measures must be clearly articulated so that consumers have options in case the care provided is not meeting their actual needs.

In sum, although some providers, insurers, and consumers resist embracing clinical outcome measures, their concerns (though understandable) can be addressed. It is well worth doing so, since the potential for outcome-oriented improvement in quality of care, and in real-life consumer recovery, will greatly benefit all parties.

Australia, a World Leader in Mental Health Outcome Measurement

In America, several states have begun experimenting with mental health outcome measurement, including Virginia (Blank, Koch, and Burkett 2004) and Ohio (Brower 2003). But other nations have gone much further, especially Australia, which is recognized as a world leader in this regard. For years Australia has been systematically collecting standardized consumer-level mental health outcome data. They have found that ongoing clinical outcome measurement is doable on a national level if it is implemented with a strategic and coordinated approach, is supported by strong leadership, and includes commitment from mental health clinicians and program managers (Pirkis et al. 2005; Whiteford and Buckingham 2005). Australia uses a battery of surveys called the Health of the Nation Outcome Scales, which generate a very valuable set of data known as the Mental Health National Outcomes and Casemix Collection.

Researchers have begun working with this collection of outcome data to determine scientifically to what extent persons with serious mental illness improve from treatment received in the public sector. Initial findings show that improvement occurs but is more variable than had been hoped. For instance, improvement among those receiving community services (as contrasted with those receiving hospital care) is below expectations (Burgess, Pirkis, and Coombs 2006).

The good news is that this finding now gives mental health policy makers in Australia something concrete to work with as they continue their efforts to reform their system of care. They can begin to identify which mental health treatments and services are most effective for which patients in the home community. In other words, they are "turning on the light" of outcome data so as to see clearly what must be done to improve care.

Not surprisingly, Burgess, Pirkis, and Coombs (2006, 7) found that their research, drawing on the Australian Mental Health National Outcomes and Casemix Collection, "demonstrates the value of routine outcome measurement, in terms of informing questions of service quality and effectiveness." If Australia can do this, so can the United States.

Recommendations

The utilization of clinical outcome measures, though not without challenges, would have a transforming impact on the quality of mental health care. Insurers and clinicians who use standardized measures in a uniform manner provide a service both to the individual consumer and to the goal of mental health system transformation. Not surprisingly, policy makers can be reluctant to move in this direction because of resistance on the part of some constituents. What would help? What steps might realistically be taken to promote much-needed outcome-based reforms? Following are specific recommendations for mental health policy makers, providers, consumers, and insurers that would jump-start the long overdue transformation of America's mental health service system.

Federal and State Mental Health Policy Makers

Policy makers must recognize that now is the time to enact legislation to transform the mental health system, even if doing so carries some political risk. Specifically, policy makers should implement legislation or regulations to

1. *Require the regular use of standardized, objective, and uniformly applied clinical outcome measures (such as NOMs) and link the availability of outcome data to continued funding.* In other words, codify the concept that programs being paid to provide mental health services should be accountable for the outcome of those services. Over time, this would have the desired effect of "turning on the light" by revealing which programs and treatments are most effective for which consumers in which settings. The actual measures selected (for both inpatient and outpatient services) and the protocol for their use should be facilitated at the federal level (e.g., SAMHSA) for uniformity so that results can be compared both within and across states. The selection of these measures should result from a collaborative process in which all constituents are invited to the table to offer input and feedback. The states must not feel that these measures are arbitrarily and autocratically imposed by the federal government. At the same time, the federal government must show real leadership and ensure that national standardized measures are indeed developed and implemented, though in a manner acceptable to all.

2. *Require the resultant transparent outcome data (aggregated and without any identifying information) to be made available.* Data should be provided to policy makers and third-party payers for reviewing the effectiveness of care across programs and to consumers for making informed decisions regarding their own treatment options. At the same time, guidelines for analysis must be developed so that differences in consumer populations and treatment settings do not lead to misinterpretation of outcome data. For instance, expected outcomes for those providers who treat persons with the most severe

types of mental illness (such as chronic paranoid schizophrenia) will be markedly different from those for providers treating primarily persons with mild-to-moderate cases of depression or anxiety disorders.

3. *Stipulate that outcome data are to be used in a remedial manner.* Specific programs or treatment services found not to be as effective as desired should be offered help in terms of technical assistance, training, and reassignment. Only after such help fails to improve outcome should consideration be given to other options such as shifting funding to more effective care.

4. *Adequately fund the cost of implementing clinical outcome measures.* A sure way for outcome measures to fail is to require them of providers without offering technical assistance and training and without providing remuneration for the added administrative costs entailed. Anyone who has evaluated a program knows that evaluation costs something. Such costs are typically included as part of overall operational expenses. Ongoing clinical outcome data collection cannot somehow magically be added without cost to the mental health service system. It must be adequately funded, with realistic allowance for training and equipment and extra time required, or it will not succeed. Furthermore, the funds must not simply come from reduction of current service rates, since this would be asking providers to cover the cost. The states will need access to federal grants in order to be able to launch systemwide mental health outcome measurement initiatives, and in like manner counties will need access to state grants. The more impoverished public systems will require even more help, such as on-site consultation and technical assistance. That said, it is hard to imagine money better spent, since the resultant information will serve to continually improve both the quality of care and the quality of life for those receiving mental health treatment.

5. *Stipulate which agency or office will regularly review and analyze the resultant clinical outcome data.* Also, stipulate how that analysis will be fed back into the system of care for quality improvement and system transformation. In the public sector, this could involve the states' departments of mental health and SAMHSA. In the private sector, it could involve insurance industry groups and mental health professional organizations.

6. *Put oversight in place to ensure that the overall result of all of the above is improved lives for persons with serious mental illness.* The whole point of measuring clinical outcomes is to make sure that those receiving care improve to the point of recovery. At both the federal and state levels this means that a person or office must be charged with overseeing the big picture and ensuring the intended outcome. Any treatments or programs found not to be effective should be given opportunity to improve, but if improvement is not forthcoming, funding should shift to more effective care. It is not compassionate to continue to fund services that accomplish little in the lives of persons with serious mental illness. It is compassionate, ethical, and rational to fund that which works.

Mental Health Providers

Providers must fully embrace the call for evidence-based practice and become competent with the use of ongoing, standardized outcome data as a means for ensuring quality of care. Specifically, providers should

1. *Move ahead now by using clinical outcome measures, rather than waiting until insurers require such data as a matter of course.* Providers must get ahead of the curve by familiarizing themselves with the outcome literature and instruments relevant to their consumers and setting. They should select an instrument to use on a trial basis in order to test the waters and broaden their experience with outcome-oriented care. There are several ways this can be done, including paying for proprietary instruments and data services or using freely available measures (see Corcoran and Fischer 2000; Corrigan, McCracken, and McNeilly 2005; Kelly 2003a). The resultant data can be used to inform case management and to maximize the effectiveness of clinical care. As noted above, consumers sometimes reveal critical issues on questionnaires that were not covered in therapy or that they were hesitant to verbalize face to face. Thus the feedback loop of clinical outcome data provides a valuable supplement to ongoing treatment and services and tends to improve the quality of care. Further, with outcome information available a provider can objectively determine early on if a case is not improving as rapidly as expected on the basis of the relevant literature and can adjust treatment accordingly.

2. *Market the fact that your practice uses scientifically validated clinical outcome measures as an indication that your services are a "cut above."* Consumers appreciate providers who use outcome measures to determine how well they are doing on a regular basis, who adjust treatment as indicated, and who thus track their wellness in confident expectation of timely improvement. They correctly conclude that such attention to results is associated with high quality care.

3. *Include the consumer's outcome data in requests for authorization for additional care (assuming full confidentiality is completely assured).* Both public and private insurers appreciate a request for additional services that is accompanied by standardized, scientific outcome information. It is easier to make a positive reauthorization decision based on clinical judgment plus data than on clinical judgment alone.

Mental Health Consumers

Consumers must see that focusing on their own clinical progress ensures a quality of care that is sadly lacking today and that this is one way to meaningfully collaborate in the treatment process. Specifically, a consumer should

1. *Regularly review your clinical status with your service provider,* as indicated on standardized outcome measures. The era of mental health care simply being prescribed by unquestioned authority is coming to an end. As the system is transformed, there will be increasing opportunities for consumers to participate in the treatment decisions that so affect their lives. A growing chorus of consumer requests for real-time clinical outcome data to ensure quality of care would help speed the adoption of outcome measures.

2. *Always ask for standardized outcome information when selecting a specific program or treatment service to make sure it's effective.* Is it an evidence-based practice? What data are available to demonstrate that this program or treatment will be able to really help the consumer, given one's particular needs at this particular time? Will outcome measures be used to help guide and individualize treatment? If the answers to these questions are not satisfactory, the consumer may want to look elsewhere.

3. *Get involved with advocacy organizations* such as the National Alliance for the Mentally Ill (www.nami.org) and Mental Health America (formerly the National Mental Health Association, www.nmha. org). This is a time of change as the current status quo system of mental health services begins to yield to reform efforts. Consumers can be a part of the transformation process by joining in advocacy efforts and by volunteering to help others who struggle with serious mental illness move to recovery.

Public- and Private-Sector Insurers

Insurers must recognize the potential for improving quality of care, as well as the bottom line, by funding only evidence-based, effective services.[9] They must also recognize that it is well worth paying more for high-quality services, including covering the additional costs entailed in measuring clinical outcomes. Specifically, insurers should

1. *Develop pilot projects to test the actual cost/benefit ratio of implementing outcome-oriented care.* Use selected standardized clinical outcome measures, drawing on the scientific literature as well as the work of relevant government agencies such as SAMHSA. The pilot should be limited to a certain geographic region (or portion of the business) and should run for perhaps six to twelve months. Assuming positive results, lessons learned could then be applied to full deployment.
2. *Move to full deployment by requiring all mental health providers to use the pilot-tested instruments and procedures.* This should include offering incentives such as preferred payment levels and recompense for administrative time required in order to boost compliance. Begin deployment with systemwide training for all involved (providers, administrators, managers, etc.). Of course, this will cost something for the insurer, but it is money well spent.
3. *Seek support (tax incentives, etc.) from relevant state government and/ or regulatory agencies for innovative mental health care.* Consider the "public-private partnership" option where appropriate, in which costs and resources of moving into outcome-oriented mental health care are shared.

4. *Market being on the "cutting edge" of high-quality care by moving into outcome-oriented services.* Take corporate pride in taking a lead role in the long-overdue transformation of mental health care. Market efforts to potential customers, who will be attracted to an insurer who is focused on achieving desired outcomes in the lives of those insured.

Conclusion

America is once again at a crossroads with her vast yet broken mental health care system. This has happened before, and always with the result of dramatic and long-lasting changes in mental health services. Over a half-century ago, in the 1950s, psychiatric hospitals across the nation were filled with hundreds of thousands of patients. Care was primarily custodial, and persons with serious mental illness such as schizophrenia could typically expect to live their lives in the confines of an institution. As we now know, life inside those psychiatric institutions was often grim.

Then an amazing thing happened. Antipsychotic medications such as Thorazine were developed and made available for the first time for hospitalized patients—especially the many thousands suffering from schizophrenia. These medications provided relief from the often terrifying symptoms of psychosis and enabled many to be discharged who otherwise would likely have been institutionalized the rest of their lives (though not without risk of tardive dyskinesia). The discharge process, which became known as "deinstitutionalization," continued for decades until the number of hospitalized patients dropped to a fraction of what it had been.

Deinstitutionalization was, and is, a compassionate mental health policy the intent of which is to enable persons with serious mental illness to live successfully in their home communities. Nobody should ever be forced to live their life in a psychiatric facility unless there is simply no other realistic alternative. However, for deinstitutionalization to succeed it is critical that consumers' home communities provide the kinds of services and supports necessary for real recovery. This was supposed to have occurred with the shift to development and expansion of community mental health centers (CMHCs) throughout the 1960s, 1970s, and 1980s. Instead, the CMHCs ended up being underfunded and in some cases poorly managed and therefore unable to provide adequate and effective care. Persons with serious mental illness were dutifully discharged from psychiatric facilities, only to fall into the cracks between the inpatient and outpatient components of America's deinstitutionalized mental health system. Tragically, many consumers to this day cycle in and out of psychiatric facilities and end up homeless. Research indicates that nearly one-third of homeless individuals have a serious mental disorder (Health Care for the Homeless Clinicians' Network 2004), an undeniable indicator of the brokenness of the current mental health system.

Thus over the past half-century the focus of mental health care has shifted from the hospital to the community, but the community has not yet succeeded in picking up the ball. Now, at the beginning of the twenty-first century, America has the opportunity to finally get it right. Many voices are calling for transformation of our broken mental health system. The national vision for reform is a good one—to create effective home- and community-based services in place of custodial hospital care and to expect recovery as the outcome of effective care. But if America is really going to transform a moribund system of mental health services, it must have the courage to put a critical missing component in place—standardized, objective clinical outcome measures uniformly applied. Without the ongoing flow of data these measures will provide, it is impossible to know to what extent community-based services are truly operational and working as intended. Once outcome data are made available, policy makers, consumers, providers, and insurers alike will be able to tell what is working, for whom, and in what setting.

It is time to "turn on the light" of clinical outcome data so that all parties can ensure that persons with serious mental illness are given the opportunity to recover in their home community and to take their place beside other productive citizens. Although a few will always be in legitimate need of hospitalization, that should be rare and should never consist of custodial care. Homelessness should be even more rare, as the streets are no place to solve the challenges of serious mental illness. Innovative, results-oriented, home- and community-based services designed for recovery are where the solutions will be found. Without standardized outcome data to guide the way by identifying those programs and services that really work, system transformation will ultimately fail, and consumers will continue to cycle in and out of hospitals and onto the streets.

"That which is measured improves." One example of this is the Continuity of Care measure currently used throughout the state of Virginia as part of the POMS approach discussed above. This measure is designed to track consumer access to community services in the local CMHCs. Before its use, access was highly variable across the counties. Some CMHCs did a pretty good job of responding rapidly to needs, but others had unreasonably long wait periods that meant consumers' needs went unmet for days or even weeks—long enough in some cases to lead to rehospitalization. Now that consumer access is measured and the results are regularly analyzed, the CMHCs are demonstrating improvement year by year. Nobody wants to look bad on a report card, so that which is measured indeed tends to get better, and everyone wins as a result.

Perhaps outcome-oriented recovery should be called the third revolution in mental health care. The first emptied the psychiatric hospitals, the second attempted (with mixed success) to provide community-based solutions through CMHCs, the third will complete the process by implementing results-oriented, home- and community-based recovery. An outcome-oriented recovery-based system of care would make caring Americans proud. It has been said that you can judge a nation by how it treats its most vulnerable citizens, and treating citizens with serious mental illness well is indeed the ethical thing for a nation to do. But it is also the most economically sensible way to deploy the many billions of dollars already dedicated to mental health services. Instead of creating dependency, outcome-oriented recovery creates opportunities for those with serious mental illness to have a real home, a satisfying job, and deep relationships. It is time to roll up our sleeves and do what it takes to transform America's broken mental health service system. The first step is to "turn on the light" of outcome data so we can see clearly where we are, where we're heading, and how best to get there.

3

Monopolies Don't Work

Simply stated, there is no inconsistency between vigorous competition and the delivery of high quality health care. Theory and practice confirm that quite the opposite is true—when vigorous competition prevails, consumer welfare is maximized in health care.

Timothy J. Muris, Chairman, Federal Trade Commission, *Everything Old Is New Again* (2002)

Antitrust policy is premised on the judgment that competitive markets, relative to other methods of allocating scarce resources, do the best job and thus make consumers as well off as possible.

Deborah Haas-Wilson, Professor of Economics, Smith College, *Managed Care and Monopoly Power* (2003)

ONE OF THE least exciting jobs of a mental health commissioner is to review and sign off on major contracts between various suppliers and the state. The contract could be for anything—food supplies or repairs for the hospitals, psychiatric medications, new computers for the central office—you name it. Every day a stack of such documents would appear on my desk, having already been reviewed and approved by the department's contracts division. The expectation was that I would simply flip quickly through the stack, sign off on the signature pages, and be done. However, I am a curious sort, and rather than just turn to the signature page I liked to at least scan through the supporting documentation that came with each contract. One day as I perused the supporting documents for a million-dollar-plus contract for remodeling work on several of the state's psychiatric facilities, I came across a word that caught my attention—"bribe." Tucked away in the back of the packet of information was a little note

stating that the contractor had been caught attempting to bribe a state official for the contract. As a new commissioner, I assumed that we would
not do business with a contractor capable of bribery, and that would be
that. Must be some mistake that the contract somehow ended up on my
desk. So began one of the many eye-opening adventures of my tenure as
mental health commissioner.

I couldn't believe my ears as I heard the following first from my contracts division, and then from my contact at the attorney general's office:

- "Yes the contractor has been caught—in fact audiotaped by the
  contracts officer who was being offered cash to ensure the deal."
  (Please note the personal integrity and initiative of the contracts
  officer who turned this in at some risk to self, only to find out that
  the deal would go ahead anyway.)
- "Yes the decision has been made to go ahead with the contract,
  since there is concern that if we do not, the contractor may successfully sue for costs incurred through the bidding process."
- The solution to the problem? (Hold your breath for this one, which
  still floors me.) "Since we have learned that the contractor is not
  trustworthy, an additional $20,000 is included to pay for close sur-
  veillance by a contracts officer throughout the work."

Any reader without government experience may think I am making this
up, and I wish I were. I was furious and refused to sign the contract despite advice from my contact at the Attorney General's Office to the contrary. Ultimately I appealed to the governor, who supported my position
and publicly recognized the courage of the contracts officer who taped
the bribe offer. The job was readvertised, and the corrupt contractor was
banned from doing service with the state for a good number of years. No
lawsuit was filed; no liability resulted.

Why do such absurdities occur, far too frequently, in government
agencies? How can such seemingly incomprehensible decisions be ex-
plained? It all goes back to the fact that a government agency is by definition a monopolistic enterprise.[1] There is no alternate department of mental
health with whom one must compete for mental health consumers. There
is therefore no pressure to perform ever more effectively and efficiently, or
to beat out the competition in pursuit of excellence. There is nobody (except perhaps a new commissioner) to complain if the agency gets taken to
the cleaners time and again. After all, it's "just government money."

The trouble is, of course, that "government money" comes from hard-working taxpayers and is intended to provide desperately needed services for persons with serious mental illness. Every dollar that is wasted on redundant administration, on poor services, or on extra fees to monitor a bribery-inclined contractor is one less dollar for mental health treatment. If public services are important, and it is clear that they are, then there should be an even greater imperative for using money well in the public sector than in the private sector. After all it is a matter not just of maximizing profit but of providing critical services for persons whose lives may well hang in the balance. Yet time and again we learn about stunning waste and mismanagement from federal and state agencies that would not be tolerated in the private sector (e.g., Stanbury and Thompson 1995). Why doesn't the private sector tolerate waste? Because by definition waste is bad business practice. In a competitive market it is always possible to lose out to the competition and even ultimately to go out of business. Any misuse of funds wastes valuable resources that could be used to improve market share through research and development, advertising, or other strategies. Thus wasting money risks ceding advantage to one's competitors, or even closing shop.

It is important to acknowledge that the private sector is no panacea, and there have been stunning cases of mismanagement such as the Enron debacle to remind us of that fact. I am sure it is possible to identify a private-sector organization that is run more poorly than a public-sector agency, but that would not change the point. The point is that certain fundamental principles and dynamics are at play in a competitive market environment that at least make it less likely for waste to be tolerated over the long haul. After all, in the Enron case the results of poor management finally took their toll, and the organization paid the ultimate price of closing shop. This can never happen to a government agency no matter how badly it is managed.

In the public sector, as currently structured, there is little or no risk, no real competition. Nobody is going to put an "Out of Business" sign on a government agency. If tasks are not completed on time, or outcomes are not as expected, one need only claim to be "underfunded." Now, it is true that many mental health agencies are underfunded, if by that we mean there are more people who need mental health services than are currently receiving care. But what about the services that are currently being provided? Are they effective? Are they efficient in their use of resources? Are those providing care and those administering the programs acting as if other people's lives depended on it? Or is there an easygoing approach to work that gets in the way of excellence? In a world without risk, the latter is found all too often. For instance, it was not unusual to find employees reading novels during office hours in the central office when I first became commissioner (something that changed quickly as we downsized unnecessary administrative positions). Such an environment leads to bureaucratization, acceptance of poor performance, and focus on increased funding as the only battle worth fighting.[2]

For these reasons, now is not the time to infuse state and federal mental health agencies with major new funds for expanding the status quo, no questions asked. The status quo, as we have noted, is broken, and new funds without new direction will only provide more of what's not working. This is a time to transform the status quo into a mental health system of care that really works. Agencies operating in a no-risk environment, and with little oversight, cannot accomplish such transformation no matter how many legislative bills are passed calling for improvements; the incentive is simply not there. The inherent monopoly of state and federal mental health agencies must be broken, much as the railroad and oil monopolies of the late 1800s had to be broken, if transformation is to proceed. This will not happen easily or without dramatic resistance from those who are committed to the status quo, just as monopolistic forces fought against antitrust efforts in the late 1800s.

Caveat: Dedicated Government Workers

It is important to state clearly that the difficulty with monopolistic government agencies comes from how those agencies are structured, not from the employees per se. There are many dedicated individuals doing very good work in state and federal agencies, including the contracts officer referenced above. In his case, he went above and beyond the call of duty to capture evidence of wrongdoing, even putting himself at risk. However, the agency with its monopolistic structure failed him in that the organization's instinctual response was to avoid risk at all cost, even if that meant working with a corrupt contractor. There are many such dedicated government workers providing and overseeing programs and services, eager to do well with the resources at hand. And there are many mental health workers eager to provide effective and compassionate care. But for the most part they labor in monopolistic organizations that lack significant incentives for excellence. Eventually, many government employees either move on or stay and get worn down by the bureaucracy. Breaking the monopoly of state and federal agencies would improve the lives not only of those receiving care but also of those providing care. Nothing is worse than a job in which one's performance matters little and accomplishes little. Every employee longs for a job in which one is challenged to do one's best and given the encouragement and resources necessary to succeed with one's mission (DePree 2004). Monopolies tend toward the former, whereas open competition (and good management) generally encourage the latter.

During my tenure as commissioner for the Virginia Department of Mental Health I had the privilege of working with some of the most talented and dedicated professionals I have ever met. These men and women managed to stand firm against the pull toward mediocrity and demanded excellence from themselves as well as from those who reported to them. It was a blessing to have them on my executive team, and they played a significant role in the mental health reforms that were implemented in Virginia. However, such executives were rare and had to have an almost Herculean ability to withstand the pressures to go along with the status quo. Further, had they been in a competitive environment they could have gone much further and faster than the monopolistic tendencies of state government allowed.

The Case for Mental Health Antitrust Law

The public-sector mental health system is somewhat analogous to monopolistic industries of the late 1800s and early 1900s, such as railroads and oil companies, in that it functions without meaningful competition. (Of course, the analogy only goes so far, since mental health agencies are not-for-profit organizations.) If a private-sector mental health provider wants to offer services that will be paid for by state or federal funds (such as Medicaid), it must contract with the state mental health agency or a subsidiary of that agency. For instance, in most states one typically contracts either with the state psychiatric facilities for inpatient services or with the Community Mental Health Centers for outpatient services. Given the fact that there are multiple contractors, why does this fail to provide the competitive environment desired? How can public mental health care be called "monopolistic" if some services are contracted to private providers?

The difficulty with this arrangement is that even though it gives the appearance of competition it lacks the main ingredient of the private sector—market forces that call for customer satisfaction, innovation, ongoing improvement and effectiveness in the face of one's competitors. If a given mental health provider is not providing particularly effective care, what happens? Do consumers switch to other providers? No, because there are no other providers—only those with whom the state has chosen to contract, usually one per service category. Does the state weed out poor providers in a relentless drive toward excellent care? No, because annual performance evaluations, if they do occur, are typically pro forma—focused more on the *process* of service delivery than the outcome. In other words, if a given provider is indeed providing the services called for in their contract it is unlikely that hard questions will be raised as to the actual outcomes of those services in the lives of those receiving care.

The reader may reasonably ask why this is so, why state oversight typically consists of only pro forma performance reviews. The answer is, once again, that there is no economic imperative to do otherwise. The state mental health agency manages little or no economic risk regarding the effectiveness of mental health care. And the political risk is minimal, since any problems can be attributed to the agency being "underfunded." Further, since few or no uniform outcome data are available across states, there is no sense of competition or comparison with other states' mental health agencies. That last point leads to one strategy for advancing mental health reform.

If state mental health agencies by definition are monopolistic because of lack of economic market forces, what can be done? It would be absurd to charter duplicative state agencies to compete with each other for the same market. So instead, why not use political "market forces" by comparing and contrasting the performance of mental health agencies across all states? Every state mental health agency reports ultimately to that state's governor, and no governor wants to look bad in contrast with other governors. Currently it would be very difficult to attempt a multistate comparison of mental health outcomes, since there is little in the way of normative, comparable data to use. But imagine what would happen if each state were required to use the same outcome measures (tailored to regions and populations), to use them regularly for all people receiving mental health care, and to publicly report the resultant data (aggregated so as to avoid any identifying information)? In that case, the

missing economic imperative would be replaced by a political imperative that would have the same result—it would drive states to do their
best lest they be seen in a poor light in contrast with their "competitor"
states.

A second reform strategy would be for state mental health agencies
to ensure that, wherever possible, they contract with multiple providers
who would be allowed to compete for a specific market of mental health
consumers seeking the same category of care. If there is only one game in
town, one provider to meet a given need, there is little incentive for innovative and efficient services. But if there are several providers offering
the same category of mental health care covered by the state, then market
forces come into play, and providers will be keenly interested in competing well to attract those consumers who need their services. It is true that
currently few private providers specialize in treating persons with serious
mental illness. But this would change if adequate funding were offered by
the state. Some argue that only state employees can adequately care for
this population, since their needs can be quite challenging. But there are
private-sector programs in the Los Angeles area, for instance, that manage
to work very well with persons with serious mental illness. One of these is
iCan, an organization that specializes in treatment for persons with severe
disabilities and contracts with the state. This organization does good work
with the most challenging population—proving it can be done. The state's
job would be to help facilitate a healthy market of potential providers and
to ensure no gaps of service as providers start up or (more rarely) pull
out.

In light of these two potential strategies, what sort of state/federal legislation or regulation would help advance competition and quality of care
in mental health services? What would mental health antitrust law actually look like?

Concerning the need for comparative data across states, consider
SAMHSA, the primary services-oriented federal mental health agency.
SAMHSA funds a small but significant portion of mental health care in
each state and could require normative outcome data for states to receive
those federal funds. States could be required to use standardized outcome
surveys developed by SAMHSA in consultation with the states, aggregate
the resultant data, and share the data with SAMHSA so that comparative information could be made available to all. This might be somewhat
unnerving for states concerned that results could be used punitively or

that the comparative information could make them look bad in contrast with other states. SAMHSA would need to stipulate that outcome data would be used only to guide technical assistance and other remedial resources and never for punitive purposes. SAMHSA would also need to acknowledge that clinical outcomes may vary for legitimate reasons, including the level of pathology being treated. For instance, metropolitan areas in warm climates typically have a higher percentage of homeless people struggling with serious mental illness such as schizophrenia than cold-climate areas. They may not be able to achieve the same average outcomes as metropolitan areas with small homeless populations. Such differences must be taken into account and duly noted in any release of data or comparative study. The potential for undue embarrassment must be reckoned with and managed well, but this is not a rationale to refuse to report standardized outcome data altogether. Rather, it is a reminder that such data must always be used in a sophisticated and fair manner, which is SAMHSA's charge.

Concerning the need for multiple providers for consumers to choose from, state legislatures could pass a bill requiring that their mental health agency contract with at least two providers for each category of service offered, in such a way as to ensure that genuine competitive market forces are in play. This may be a little less efficient initially, since recruitment of multiple providers may not always be easy. In some cases, it may be necessary to first invest in creating a fiscal and contracting environment within which multiple innovative mental health providers can develop and compete. But in the long run, once such an environment is in place and providers are competing for the privilege of providing care, service quality will improve and costs will be kept reasonable by market forces.

How Market Competition Helps Mental Health Care

Some may be skeptical as to whether market forces can really work in the realm of mental health care and whether they would actually improve the quality of care or simply enrich a few savvy providers. There is a growing literature addressing such questions, including *Managed Care and Monopoly Power*, written by Deborah Haas-Wilson, professor of economics at Smith College. Haas-Wilson found that a competitive mental health market requires five factors:

1. *Well-informed consumers.* Mental health consumers must be able to learn about the quality and cost of services offered by various providers.
2. *Price-sensitive consumers.* There must be incentive to search for mental health providers who offer the best service for the time and resources spent.
3. *Well-informed sellers.* Mental health providers must know about their customers, their needs and preferences.
4. *Easy market entry and exit.* It must be fairly easy for mental health providers to enter profitable markets and exit unprofitable ones.
5. *Avoidance of monopoly.* There must be an option for competitive mental health providers to enter the market and offer similar services at lower cost and/or higher rate of effectiveness.

If any one of these conditions is not met, then the benefits of market competition are compromised. If several are not met, as is the case in most if not all states, then market benefits are lost altogether. But why is that so? What is so important about each of these areas that without them the mental health care system suffers? To answer that question, let us consider each of these five areas in terms of case examples.[3] What does all this mean in the actual lives of people struggling with serious mental illness?

Well-Informed Consumers

The first time an individual experiences a mental health crisis is often confusing, frightening, and isolating. It is confusing because most people don't really know what constitutes a depression or anxiety disorder or other mental illness. It may initially seem like simple mood changes, only to explode into an array of symptoms that totally disrupt life at work or school or home. It is frightening because there is no way to make it go away, to know how long it will last, or to know whether life will ever be "normal" again. It is isolating because despite gains made over the last generation, mental illness is still stigmatized, and friends and family typically prefer to ignore it as long as possible. Consequently, individuals or their families may find themselves under pressure to make quick decisions without really knowing much about what they are dealing with or what their options are. Unfortunately, hasty and ill-informed decisions can lead to tragic outcomes when they concern serious mental illness.

"SUSAN"

Dr. Robb was head of a well-known nonprofit organization in Washington, D.C., and his wife served as a fundraiser. Their beautiful sixteen-year-old daughter and only child, Susan, was the shining star in her parents' life. She excelled in school and sports, had many good friends, and had managed to avoid the "rebellious" stage many teens seem destined to go through. So it was hard to know what to do when Susan began withdrawing from her friends, performing poorly in school, and behaving oddly at home. She even spoke of hearing voices telling her awful things. Her parents first assumed this was her version of rebellion and responded by gently but firmly redirecting her to maintain her "mature behavior" regardless of how she might feel. Surely this was a phase that would pass, and it was no time to publicly embarrass a prominent family. Like most parents, they knew little about serious mental illness and had no occasions to learn in the midst of their busy professional lives. Also, like most families, they were very reluctant to admit to themselves that it could even be possible for their child to become mentally ill.

Unfortunately, despite an initial brave attempt to recover lost ground, Susan became ever more desperate as she wrestled with what seemed to be strange demons that nobody else acknowledged or understood. Then she did something nobody could ignore. Obeying voices that became ever more persistent, she made a suicide attempt by taking several bottles' worth of various prescription medications and ended up hospitalized. This led to a series of physical and psychological evaluations, resulting in a conclusion that nobody wanted to hear. Susan had had a psychotic break and was suffering from schizophrenia.

At this point Susan's parents were desperate to quickly find something that would make the nightmare go away. Their daughter's emotional pain, combined with the pressure to rapidly resolve family difficulties that most public professionals feel, led them to jump at the first option they came across. So they did what most people do—they went to see the first mental health professional they could find. In this case it was a psychiatrist, recommended by a friend, who specialized in treating government officials and their families. The psychiatrist assessed Susan and prescribed pharmacotherapy—an antipsychotic medication. This helped minimize the voices but left her feeling like she was living in an emotional straitjacket. It also led to rapid weight gain that was troubling to Susan, who had always been athletically inclined. She could not feel or think clearly, she became overweight and listless, and her mood plummeted. In response, she was put on antidepressant medications as well, which seemed to help her mood but also led to unwanted side effects such as sleep disturbance. This led to more medications to help her sleep. After about six months of treatment Susan again tried to take her life by swallowing a potent mix of her various prescription medications.

This time her parents understood what had eluded them before—that serious mental illness is a very complex challenge that must be met with careful decisions based on the very best information. They also understood that what the market readily offers, the treatments typically made available, may not be what's needed. They began researching treatments for schizophrenia and discovered that overmedication is a typical but unhelpful response.[4] They found that specialization matters and that their provider was not a specialist in adolescent care or in schizophrenia. They evaluated various treatment programs and found that the most effective treatment involves a combination of medication and innovative psychotherapy provided by a trusted therapist who is involved in daily life when needed—not just limited to a weekly or monthly office visit. They found to their sorrow that people rarely recover from schizophrenia, that it usually lasts a lifetime. But they also found that with effective treatment—"evidence-based practice"—it is possible to manage schizophrenia well such that it need not keep an individual from living a rich, full, successful life. Susan ended up finding a psychiatrist with whom she connected well, with expertise in adolescent care as well as schizophrenia, and who focused more on therapy than on medication. Susan ended up developing a new approach to life altogether that involved managing her mental illness with minimal (although still significant) medication, stress management strategies, and ongoing support from her therapist.

How does all this affect the market? Since even sophisticated, professional people such as Susan's parents know little about mental illness or what constitutes effective treatment, there is little market demand for the best care—for evidence-based practices. Most individuals and their families assume that whatever treatment approach they stumble onto in the midst of their crisis will be sufficient. They are confused and frightened and are simply glad to find a mental health professional or program that seems to know what's needed. Unfortunately, that's not good enough. Too many mental health professionals provide the treatments they are most comfortable with, usually what they were taught in graduate school, rather than the current evidence-based practice that might best fit the need of the patient. If the market for mental health services were driven by well-informed consumers demanding innovative, effective, evidence-based practices, this would change. Providers would respond by learning and offering what their patients most need, and the average quality of care would improve accordingly.

For this to occur, effort needs to be made to educate potential mental health consumers as to what their options are and what tends to be most effective for a given mental illness. In the private sector, some insurance companies are now offering help in the form of a benefits counselor who works with the individual needing mental health care until she has found the right treatment. This is to avoid a waste of time and money that benefits neither the patient nor the insurer. In the public sector, there are mental health advocates who serve a similar role. In both cases, the result is a better-informed consumer who is therefore more likely to find effective care, which benefits all parties. State legislatures should consider requiring such services in both the public and private sectors, knowing that the result will be improved quality of care and less "down time" for those struggling with serious mental illness.

Price-Sensitive Consumers

The next question that faces a person with serious mental illness, after locating a mental health treatment option, is how to pay for it. Many individuals have health insurance policies and thus have private-sector resources to draw on, at least until their benefits run out. Others have no such insurance and must rely on public-sector funds such as state psychiatric hospitals and community mental health centers. Unfortunately, in neither case are the consumers attentive to the cost of care.

For those with health insurance, a lot depends on what sort of coverage is included for mental health care. In many cases, the coverage is not very good and in fact is significantly less than that provided for physical health care. For instance, a person may be eligible for thirty days' hospital stay per year for physical needs, but only seven days per year for mental health needs. This often means that mental health benefits are quickly exhausted with a bout of serious mental illness. Ultimately, the solution is to work on "parity" benefits, which means that coverage for mental health care should equal coverage for physical health care. Thankfully, Congress passed a mental health parity law in 2007 that will begin to address this need. But with or without parity, it is important to note that most people who have insurance do not spend a lot of time shopping for the best treatment value for their insurance dollars. It is assumed that such matters will be worked out between the provider and the insurer and that there is no point to trying to locate particularly cost-efficient mental health providers. This is unfortunate, since it means that insured mental health consumers are not particularly price-sensitive—at least not until their insurance runs out and they are paying out of pocket. Consequently, most mental health providers face little or no scrutiny from their insured patients as to how their fees may compare with competitors'.

Of course, insurance companies negotiate rates with their preferred providers, but this does not provide the same benefit. The company is simply interested in getting the lowest rate possible and drives a hard bargain that may or may not lead to reasonably priced high-quality care. Too often, it simply leads to underpaid providers who are not particularly motivated to go the extra mile on behalf of their insured patients. Instead, and understandably, the preference is for self-pay patients who can pay full rate out of pocket. What is needed is for the individual insured patients to be empowered to find effective care at reasonable prices. One way to do this would be for those insured to be able to apply their full benefit amount to any qualified provider—a sort of health care voucher system. In fact, some policy makers have suggested that the use of health care vouchers in and of itself would help reform the health care system (e.g., Emanuel and Fuchs 2005).

For those without insurance, and who meet whichever means test may be applicable, there is the public-sector mental health system consisting of state psychiatric hospitals and community mental health centers. Here too, the individual seeking care is not likely to ask questions as to the cost or efficiency of care. After all, the services are covered by either state or federal funds. This is of course a blessing for those receiving needed care, but the lack of price sensitivity is unfortunate in that public sector patients provide no imperative for cost efficiencies. As with the private-sector example, the use of vouchers could be helpful. For example, the state could introduce a voucher system giving public-fund-eligible patients a certain amount to draw on per year for treating their mental illness. The amount could vary based on diagnosis, severity, and average cost of local mental health services. There could be a review and appeals system in place to handle unique cases. Vouchers would help mental health consumers to become more price conscious, since they would see the cost of care, and as a result the market would respond by promoting an array of competitive providers. Without this or some other mechanism allowing for price-sensitive consumers, the public-sector mental health market can be expected to remain largely free from competitive market forces—forces that would provide an imperative for continual quality improvement.

"SAM"

Sam was a twenty-seven-year-old itinerant laborer who had a growing drinking problem and was often unemployed. Over the past five years he had found himself moving from social "happy hour" drinking, to serious booze parties, to binge drinking alone at home. His current employer was sympathetic but made it clear that he had to get his alcoholism under control if he wanted to keep his job, which he had only recently acquired. Reluctantly, Sam checked himself into a residential treatment program, expecting to stay the full thirty-day term as advertised. Instead, he found that his benefits ran out after seven days, and he was discharged with instructions to attend a local Alcoholics Anonymous (AA) group. He did so for a few weeks but then found himself once again binge drinking. He attempted to check himself into a state psychiatric hospital that offered a well-regarded drug treatment program but was turned down since he was not a "threat to self or others."[5] Despondent, Sam began drinking more heavily than ever and once again lost his job. He then got in a violent barroom fight that led to jail and a psychological evaluation, which determined he had now become a "threat to others." This meant he was finally eligible for admission to the state hospital that had turned him away previously, and he was admitted to their thirty-day treatment program.

Sam experienced both private-sector and public-sector mental health coverage problems, since his insurance benefits were quickly exhausted. This is not unusual, given the poor level of mental health coverage offered in many health insurance plans. It could be said that, functionally, many private insurers shift mental health costs to the public sector in this manner. But equally important is the fact that in neither scenario— private or public—did Sam care about the cost of care he was receiving. It made no difference to him whether his insurance dollars, or later his Medicaid dollars, were being well spent. He didn't even bother to find out what any given treatment cost. This means that the market for mental health providers is deprived of the healthy dynamic of cost-sensitive consumers. Most consumers are very concerned about finding appropriate care but little concerned about the cost as long as private or public funds are available.

The only exception to this rule is the small number of patients who decide to pay out of pocket for one reason or another. Perhaps they are too wealthy to meet the Medicaid means test, yet have no insurance. Perhaps they prefer to keep their care "off the books" and thus not to have to acknowledge treatment for mental illness if asked by a potential employer. Or perhaps their insurance ran out in the middle of treatment and they decided to pay for the completion on their own. In such circumstances consumers become all too aware of the cost of care, but even then they may not spend time doing a cost-benefit analysis comparing the fees and effectiveness (actual clinical outcomes) of various providers.

What can be done? As suggested above, vouchers could be used to help bring price sensitivity on a large scale to both private-sector and public-sector consumers. The voucher constitutes a sufficient but limited resource that can be individually managed by the consumer as he or she sees fit (with an appeals process for exceptional cases). With vouchers in place, mental health providers would of course be asked how much they charge for various services, and this could be compared with the provider down the road. Effective providers offering reasonable rates would be rewarded with increasing shares of the market. In other words, there would be a viable imperative for mental health providers to become more ever more effective and efficient so as to be able to attract more patients seeking cost-effective high-quality care.

State legislatures should consider calling for pilot projects to test the helpfulness of vouchers for mental health care in both private-sector and public-sector settings.[6]

Well-Informed Sellers

Thankfully, many mental health providers know quite a lot about their patients—their backgrounds and diagnoses, their needs and preferences, and their response to treatment. Many psychiatrists, psychologists, and social workers, as well as program managers, listen carefully to those coming for mental health services and do their best to meet individuals' needs with compassionate and effective care. But in my experience I have found that too many do not. Too many think they already know best what a given patient needs, ignore evidence-based practices (sometimes called "best practices"), and pay little or no attention to what the individual or their family may request. In a noncompetitive market most patients don't have much of a choice. They must work with whatever provider is available even if they have reservations about the service provided. This means that competitive market forces are not in play and that, as a result, the quality of care suffers. What's needed is a market environment that encourages mental health providers to pay careful attention to the specific needs and preferences of each patient, to learn applicable evidence-based practices as they become available, and to monitor the outcomes of their treatment to ensure top-quality care.

"DR. JONES"

Dr. Jones was a psychologist practicing in the Washington, D.C., area who had received his doctorate in clinical psychology from a major university in the 1980s. While there, he learned that a person suffering from the trauma of a sexual assault must always have opportunity to talk it through in detail so as to be able to "move on" psychologically. When Evelyn, a thirty-two-year-old single professional who worked as a staffer in a senator's office, came to him for help with depression, she mentioned in passing what he concluded must be the core of her problems—a sexual assault. Seventeen years previously, as a teenager, she had been assaulted by a cousin visiting her family. She had seen a counselor at the time and did not think about it much any more. She claimed that her depression was related to more current events such as being trapped in a dead-end job, coupled with a recent breakup with her fiancé. She was having a hard time sleeping and eating, was crying daily, was plagued with the thought that she was a "nobody," was not functioning well at work, and wanted speedy relief. She was not interested in taking antidepressant medications, but she had heard that a new approach to psychotherapy known as cognitive-behavioral therapy typically helped patients overcome depression within six to twelve weeks and wanted to try it if possible.

Dr. Jones, however, had a different perspective. He too had heard about cognitive-behavioral therapy, but he had not been able to take the training needed to become proficient with this new short-term approach to psychotherapy. He had learned "psychoanalytic psychotherapy," which focuses on the long-term exploration of deep issues, often tracing back to childhood sexual experiences. Putting this together with the fact that Evelyn was the survivor of a sexual assault, he concluded that she needed long-term psychoanalytic psychotherapy, beginning with a full recounting of her experiences during the assault.

Evelyn had misgivings about such an approach, but Dr. Jones was one of the few approved mental health providers listed on her HMO insurance plan who lived in walking distance, and she didn't own a car. So she decided to go ahead with the recommended treatment. Unfortunately, focusing on her assault had the opposite of the intended effect—it made things worse, and her depression deepened. In fact, current evidence-based practice recognizes that for some victims of trauma it is not necessary—and may even be harmful—for them to have to "relive" the event (Devilly, Gist, and Cotton 2006). In those cases, the individual has already sufficiently processed the trauma and has appropriately moved on. However, Dr. Jones was basing his treatment decisions on what he had learned twenty years previously. He was not listening to or learning from his patient. He was not keeping up with changes in the field of psychological treatments. He was not well informed.

After four sessions Evelyn dropped out of treatment with Dr. Jones and sought a therapist trained in the short-term therapy she had heard about. Unfortunately, this meant having to pay out of pocket, since the cognitive-behavioral therapist was not on her insurance company's preferred provider list. The economic burden was significant, but within eight weeks her depression had significantly lifted and she was able to again function well at work.

Why wasn't Dr. Jones better informed both as to the type of treatment his patient wanted and needed and as to the need to evaluate a trauma victim carefully before recommending recounting the event? Because there was no economic imperative for him to do so. Insurance companies know little about what therapists actually do. They may survey their preferred providers on what approaches to treatment are offered, but research has shown that there is often little correlation between what a provider checks off on a list of treatment approaches and what is actually done during the therapy hour. The latter tends to be driven more by what the therapist learned in graduate school or has become most comfortable with since.

Further, it is difficult for patients to "shop around" and evaluate mental health providers to find a professional who clearly understands them and who will provide the most effective treatment possible. Many insurers do not cover costs for more than one initial visit, and many consumers find that only a few approved mental health providers are available to them anyway (sometimes only one).

What is needed is for both the patients and the payers to have high expectations that mental health providers will do what it takes to stay well informed so as to ensure effective and high-quality care. This means providers must keep up with the field and take training in new treatment approaches when relevant, as well as listen carefully to the patient's perspective so as to provide whatever best matches the patient's unique needs and preferences. If a provider does not happen to have the expertise a given patient requires, that patient should be referred to someone who does. Yet the current market and economic imperative pulls the other way. It is all too easy to hold onto mental health patients as long as possible, even if treatment does not seem to be helping as much as expected. To change this dynamic, the market needs to reward those providers who work hard to make sure that all patients get the most effective and efficient care possible, even if that means referring out. Identifying effective clinicians requires them to supply information on the type and duration of services provided, the actual clinical outcomes in the lives of the patients, the extent to which the provider refers to other specialists, and the effort made to keep well trained in evidence-based practices (e.g., continuing education courses). Such information can be made available to potential patients (e.g., via the Web), who can then make informed decisions as to who would likely best meet their needs.

This could be accomplished by state legislatures phasing in such requirements over several years for those seeking licensure as a mental health professional. During the phase-in time, states could offer technical assistance and training for providers, ensuring that meeting the requirements would not be overly burdensome. Some providers may see such requirements as intrusive, but many others would welcome the opportunity to increase treatment effectiveness and quality of care. In the long run, both the seller (therapist) and the buyer (patient) would benefit from being well informed. For this would improve both the quality of mental health care and the general reputation of psychological services and would invariably increase the demand for such services.

Easy Market Entry and Exit

For innovative treatments and programs to be made available, it must be fairly easy for mental health providers to enter profitable markets and exit unprofitable ones (yet without disrupting care). In other words, the mental health services market needs to be able to attract and keep talent if it is going to offer high-quality care.

In the public sector, most state mental health agencies have a Byzantine contracting process that precludes anything ever moving quickly either in or out of the market. The sheer amount of paperwork involved, which is continually being modified with new regulations or requirements for contractors, can be mind-boggling. It is not unusual for applicants to begin the process, become overwhelmed with the rigidity and complexity of the state's paperwork, and drop out rather than dedicate precious resources to something that may not be all that profitable in the first place.

The paperwork requirement is typically better in the private sector but can still be quite burdensome. Also, many insurance companies have closed their lists of preferred providers altogether and are not interested in signing on more mental health professionals. New professionals moving into the area and offering the latest evidence-based treatments need not apply.

The net effect in both the public and private sector is to discourage innovation and state-of-the-art care. Those who thrive in such stultifying environments tend to be individuals and businesses that are comfortable with the way things have always been done and that can spend a great deal of time filling out forms and "working the system"—time that could perhaps be better spent learning new evidence-based treatment approaches and thus improving the quality of care offered.

"TOM"

Tom was a young psychologist who also had business savvy,
having completed an MBA and having worked for a large mental
health care service provider. He saw the need for a new approach
to treating serious mental illness, based on providing in-home
and community services rather than always expecting the
patient to come in for weekly visits. Research had demonstrated
the effectiveness of "home- and community-based care" (e.g.,
Drake 1998) for those who do not respond well to traditional
treatment—especially homeless people with serious mental
illness. Living in a large metropolitan area with a huge homeless
population, Tom was sure that a new approach to treatment would
help many successfully get off the streets and back into their home
communities and that it could be done in a profitable manner for
reasonable cost.

So he contacted the Department of Mental Health, was
referred to the contracting division, and began a long and tortuous
process that eventually sapped his desire to do business with
the state. The forms sent to him (by e-mail attachment or to be
downloaded from various state Web sites) seemed endless and
contradictory. He would spend a lot of time drafting a business
plan, budget, and services presentation to meet state criteria,
only to find that those criteria had shifted because of new agency
regulations. Finally he completed an application packet for a
specific "Request for Proposal" (RFP) that seemed to fit his vision,
only to find that the window for applications had closed earlier
than expected.[7] He called or met with dozens of department
employees searching for someone who would support his desire
to offer innovative, state-of-the-art services for people who
were homeless and mentally ill. Instead, he found many tired
voices whose primary interest seemed to be to explain the state's
procedures and to avoid the headache of anything that challenged
the status quo.

Eventually, Tom gave up. He continued to work as a mental
health provider but regretted not being allowed the opportunity
to offer a new approach to care that could have made such a
difference in the lives of those with serious mental illness.

What would help? Streamlined contracting processes designed not to discourage innovation but to support creative new ideas for helping persons with serious mental illness recover their ability to live successfully in their home community. Department success should be measured not simply by how much funding the state provides, or how many contracts are let, but more importantly by how effective their programs are in bringing recovery to those who come in need. For that to happen, innovation must be welcomed as a friend, not shunned as a threat.

In both the public and private sectors of mental health care, this requires visionary leadership. If the CEO, or commissioner, has a vision for providing innovative and effective evidence-based community services, it can happen. Dynamic leadership can provide the imperative that current market forces lack to change structures so that creative entrepreneurs can enter and exit the market as needed. When that happens, innovative and entrepreneurial clinicians will step forward with new treatments and services for persons with serious mental illness. Those clinicians who provide high-quality creative care will be rewarded with an ever-growing market share. Those who don't will find their dwindling market share forcing them to either improve services or cease current efforts and move on to other opportunities.

Avoidance of Monopoly

There must be an option for competitive mental health providers to enter the market and offer similar services at lower cost and/or higher rate of effectiveness. This is of course the key point of a nonmonopolistic market—that several providers can openly and fairly compete for the same customers. By so doing, market forces help ensure that services as effective and efficient as possible. A strong message must be given to all involved in the mental health care delivery system that monopolistic behavior will not be tolerated. There must be legal risk, both in the public sector and in the private sector, for those who would unfairly hinder the competition so as to protect market share or maximize profits. Antitrust laws must be enforced.

According to Haas-Wilson (2003), the enforcement of antitrust laws must be carefully managed. She notes that antitrust enforcement must not be either too vigorous or too lenient. Ironically, either extreme has the same result—fewer providers will compete. If antitrust laws are only leniently enforced, then monopolistic tendencies prevail and services will be offered only by a few large organizations that work hard to keep others out of the market. On the other hand, if antitrust laws are enforced with too much zeal, then potentially cost-effective providers may be scared off entering the market for fear of frivolous litigation. Either way, the service system is left with too few providers for healthy competition. Thus it is necessary that antitrust laws be in place and be appropriately enforced, but it is critical that enforcement be managed with wisdom. The goal after all is not just to enforce the law per se but to ensure that a competitive mental health care market thrives, producing high-quality services that are as effective as they are efficient.

A VIRGINIA CASE

During my tenure as commissioner for the Virginia Department of Mental Health, I saw firsthand how monopolistic tendencies can keep expensive service providers in place. As I reviewed costs at one of the state's fifteen psychiatric facilities, I found that one had a contract with a local psychologist to provide psychological assessment services. This was something I was familiar with as a practicing psychologist, and the price seemed unusually high. So I asked about it and was told that the facility was not confident anyone else could do the job correctly, since the residents could be very difficult to work with. Consequently, even though this was a contracted service, it was essentially monopolistic. No other potential providers were ever invited to compete. Not surprisingly, the cost per assessment was rising substantially each year. Upon my instruction, the facility put out a Request for Proposal and was surprised to find that others in the area were quite capable of providing quality assessments for significantly less, thus freeing up funds for other unmet needs. The problem was not a lack of willing providers to compete for the job but the facility's monopolistic mind-set that led them to believe that the easiest approach was to find a favored provider and stick with that one indefinitely. The result? Providers often took the facility to the cleaners, assuming that once selected they were free to pass on rapid cost increases.

What would help? In both the private and public sectors what is needed is leadership that is committed to open and fair competition and willing to push that agenda. The CEO of an insurance company or the commissioner of a state department of mental health must be convinced that competitive market forces will improve quality of care and that the battle to overcome monopolistic tendencies is worth the fight. A few half-hearted efforts will not accomplish much, but a sustained effort over several years will. The Virginia Department of Mental Health contracting division came to know that it had to submit the results of a truly competitive Request for Proposal if it wanted approval. Otherwise the paperwork would be returned unsigned with instruction to do what it took to ensure a competitive response, including multiple potential providers.

Of course, in many cases this is easier said than done. At another Virginia facility located in a more rural area it was initially very difficult to find providers willing to respond to a Request for Proposal for various support services. Initial responses were discouraging, and the contracting staff wanted to revert to the sole-source contracts they were used to. Instead, we created a work group to develop a plan for eliciting new providers and helping them put in a bid. This was somewhat time consuming and costly at first, but eventually it led to an environment within which multiple qualified providers competed fairly for support services. The result? Quality of services improved, while costs remained contained or even in some cases lessened.

It is thus ultimately up to whoever is responsible for selecting leadership to determine whether monopoly will be avoided. In state government it is typically the governor who appoints the mental health commissioner. In the private sector it is typically the board that selects the CEO. Whoever has such responsibility should include a line of questions for candidates that will determine how committed they are to creating an economic environment within with healthy competition can occur. Without it, high-quality care at reasonable costs will not be attained.

Research shows that vigorous competition is in fact related to quality health care (Haas-Wilson 2003; Muris 2002). Thus to ensure that these five factors are in place is to ensure that mental health services will be more effective, with the chief benefit going to mental health consumers. If one or more of these factors is missing, then the benefit of competitive market forces is compromised. It may seem unusual to put it this way, but anyone interested in the well-being of persons struggling with serious mental illness should pay attention to the market for clinical services needed to achieve recovery. Are all five market factors in place to produce a healthy economic environment within which innovative and effective treatments and services can thrive? If not, what needs to be changed? It is just as important to advocate for an open service delivery market as it is to advocate for adequate mental health care funding. Both are needed, but without a competitive market new funds will not accomplish much.

Conclusion

Monopolies do not work in health care, any more than they did with the railroads of the late nineteenth and early twentieth centuries. All they do is produce a lot of wealth for a few, while depriving consumers of having any real choices among providers. It is natural for monopolies to develop, since those in power are bound to try to expand and consolidate their hold on the market. Who among us is selfless enough to invite others to compete for our business? This is why President Theodore Roosevelt and others, in the early 1900s, decided that the nation as a whole had to address the issue. For democracy to succeed, the open competitive market must be protected from our own monopolistic instincts lest the most powerful and successful among us take it over to the detriment of everyone else. Ultimately, it is up to us all to see to it that that does not happen. We must see to it that the laws of the land favor healthy competition and punish willful monopolies.

In the case of monopolistic mental health care the consequences are particularly severe, since most people struggling with serious mental illness have little recourse other than to accept the treatment offered. Expensive, ineffective care simply adds to the significant burden of mental illness and in some cases can be the final straw. It can push people to give up on treatment altogether, choosing instead to try to manage their symptoms on their own, or perhaps to deny that they need care at all. Too often this ends up in tragic situations such as homelessness, cyclical hospitalization, or even suicide.

The problem of a noncompetitive market is therefore not just an academic or economic question. Monopolistic mental health care is also an ethical issue. How can we in good conscience sit back while providers offer ineffective and expensive services, when we know how devastating that can be in the lives of those receiving care? Do we not owe those among us who are impaired by serious mental illness the best care that can reasonably be provided? What if it were us or our own family members? Would we be satisfied with the broken status quo mental health service delivery system? Obviously not, and just as obviously this is a matter that must be addressed with an ethical imperative.

For the sake of all Americans with serious mental illness, let us determine to do away with the monopolistic stranglehold over mental health care with the same zeal with which railroad monopolies were overcome a century ago. This means legislators and lawmakers at many levels of government need to put the need for competitive mental health services on the agenda for public discourse and for action. They must do whatever it takes to overcome the current monopolistic status quo of mental health services. Only then will we find the ability to offer a full array of competitive, innovative, effective, community-based, and reasonably priced services that will do the job. Only then will mental health providers have the benefit of working in an environment that fully supports innovation and excellence. Only then will persons with serious mental illness find the services they need to recover—to become successful members of their home community with real homes, fulfilling jobs, and deep relationships.

4

Fair Is Fair

Parity for Mental Health Coverage

I believe [this bill] sets the stage for us to enact a national policy that will ensure individuals with mental illness have parity between mental health coverage and medical and surgical coverage. It is a matter of simple fairness.

> Senator Pete Domenici, September 17, 2007,
> press release celebrating the passage of an
> expanded mental health parity bill in the U.S. Senate

No longer will we allow mental health to be treated as a stepchild in the health-care system.

> Senator Pete Domenici, after the mental health parity bill
> was signed into law by President Bush on October 3, 2008

[Imposing limits on mental health and addiction coverage is] bad medicine, bad law, and bad insurance.

> James Purcell, CEO, Blue Cross Blue Shield of Rhode Island

"TED AND JOAN"

Ted and Joan thought they had prepared well to meet any and all needs for their family of four. They both had stable, good-paying professional jobs in the Washington, D.C., area, and they owned a nice three-bedroom home in a quiet neighborhood. They had dutifully taken care of their wills, making sure that trusts were in place to avoid estate taxes, and they had excellent benefits from Ted's employer, which included generous health care coverage for the entire family. They felt as if they were prepared for anything life could throw at them. What could possibly go wrong?

Unfortunately, their teenage son—Jon—discovered the answer when he developed a serious mental illness. It began with short-term depressive episodes that kept him home from school but soon escalated into violent confrontations with his younger brother at home and with classmates at school. This triggered a referral to the school psychologist for assessment, which revealed that Jon had in fact been struggling with chronic major depression—including thoughts of suicide. Further, unbeknownst to his parents he had been "cutting" himself for some time. He had been scraping his upper arm with a needle until it bled, leaving a growing trail of scars and open wounds. But since it was done on an area that was always covered by shirtsleeves, nobody had noticed. Because of the risk of suicide, the school psychologist strongly recommended inpatient treatment.

Ted and Joan were highly motivated to find effective care for their son, and through their insurance company located a psychiatric hospital that included an adolescent wing. Given their coverage, Jon was easily admitted and began a treatment program for depressed adolescents. After five days of treatment, which consisted primarily of group psychotherapy and starting on antidepressant medication, Jon seemed to be doing much better and was discharged with instruction to seek follow-up outpatient care. He did so and began meeting with both a psychologist (for psychotherapy) and a psychiatrist (for antidepressant medication) who were on the insurance company's very limited preferred provider list. Unfortunately treatment did not seem to help, Jon began spiraling down, and his cutting came back with a vengeance. When Ted and Joan came home to find him nearly covered in blood, they took him back to the hospital for readmission on an emergency basis. After two days, they received a call that surprised them. Yes their son needed additional inpatient treatment, but their coverage, which allowed for no more than seven days per year, had run out. Jon needed additional inpatient treatment, but the cost (about $800 per day) would need to be covered out of pocket. Ted and Joan, like many who care for family members with serious mental illness, decided to spare no expense to provide whatever Jon needed. They used most of their savings to cover the nearly $10,000 bill that resulted from an additional twelve days in the hospital.

Unfortunately, this did not solve the problem. Over the period of the next three years, Jon found himself in a vicious cycle. He would seemingly respond well to inpatient treatment, be discharged, then spiral downward, only to eventually again begin cutting himself. Once the cutting became obvious, he would end up rehospitalized. As this continued Ted and Joan did all they could to help their beleaguered son, even taking out a home equity loan to cover the tens of thousands of dollars in hospital fees.

They then came to a point that is reached by many families who struggle with serious mental illness. They realized that the mental health system of care, even with insurance coverage, was itself broken and not particularly helpful for their son. So they started over, seeking new treatment providers even if they were not on their insurance company's preferred provider list. They came with high expectations and tough questions for anyone who would treat their son and ended up scheduling a trial session with me through the clinic I directed. After the first two sessions it seemed that Jon and I were working well together, so we began a course of intensive cognitive-behavioral therapy. We focused first on making sure that any depressive tendencies were addressed early on—before cutting began. Since I was not on their preferred provider list, they had to pay out of pocket for my services. But thankfully treatment went well, and Jon did not require any more hospitalization. He came to better understand the source of his emotional pain, developed strategies for managing it well, and began to once again blossom as a healthy adolescent.

Though this story eventually had a good outcome, the cost to the family was enormous both emotionally and financially. Ted and Joan aged rapidly as they attempted to manage the vicious cycle of their son's many hospitalizations over a three-year period. And they exhausted every financial resource available to them in the process. Their insurance coverage had doomed them from the start, since their inpatient benefits were very limited compared to physical health coverage. With only seven days of inpatient care allowed per year, it is predictable that anyone experiencing serious mental illness will quickly exhaust benefits and end up paying out of pocket. It is also predictable that a tightly restricted list of preferred mental health providers will not be able to meet the needs of every patient who comes for help.

What Ted and Joan needed was health insurance that would have provided as much coverage for mental health needs as for physical health needs (say, up to four weeks of inpatient care per year). They also needed for their outpatient coverage to be more flexible so that they could work with whichever psychologist or psychiatrist would be best for their son. Instead, they endured a hellacious period in their family's life that can never be forgotten and paid a heavy price for seeking help through a broken mental health system. This must always be remembered when mental health policy is being discussed. Poor policies are not just academically regrettable. They hurt real people and their families, sometimes grievously, sometimes irreparably. There must be a sense of urgency as policy makers struggle to get it right, knowing that every delay produces more tragedies for those struggling with serious mental illness. Parity is more than a dry discussion of insurance benefits. It is an ethical issue, since it determines whether individuals and families will have coverage for what they desperately need when struggling with a serious mental illness.

Parity Defined

What exactly is meant by mental health parity? There are many definitions on the market, but parity is best defined as "benefits for mental health diagnoses matching benefits for medical/surgical diagnoses in terms of service limits, cost sharing, and annual or lifetime spending limits."

Benefits refers to either private-sector (insurance) or public-sector (government aid) coverage. *Mental health diagnoses* refers to emotional disorders as defined in the *Diagnostic and Statistical Manual of Mental Disorders* (American Psychiatric Association 2000). *Service limits* refers to provider or program limitations, such as having to select from a preferred provider list. *Cost sharing* refers to out of pocket expenses such as co-pays and deductibles. *Annual or lifetime spending limits* refers to issues such as limit on number of inpatient days or outpatient visits per year. Put most simply, parity means that people seeking treatment for mental health needs should have the same resources to draw on that they would have for physical health care needs.

Insurers historically have been reluctant to cover mental health and substance abuse services on a par with general medical and surgical services because of concerns about "adverse selection" and "moral hazard." *Adverse selection* refers to the tendency for more comprehensive insurance plans to attract individuals most in need of care, thus increasing costs for the insurer. *Moral hazard* refers to some patients' tendency to overutilize services for which they do not need to pay, seeking out care that is unnecessary and/or ineffective. This is of course a concern with any form of health care coverage, but some research suggests that it is particularly so for mental health services. The Rand Health Insurance Experiment (Newhouse 1999) demonstrated that some mental health patients do tend to overuse services if coverage allows. Consequently, this is one reason that health plans have typically required higher co-pays and deductibles for mental health services (Office of the Surgeon General 1999).

Nonetheless, the plight of families such as Ted and Joan's has begun to move policy makers to consider increasing coverage for mental health services. During the 1980s, for instance, many states enacted mandates requiring insurers to cover mental health care and to offer freedom of choice among providers. However, these insurers typically imposed higher cost sharing or more restrictive benefit limits for mental health services than for general medical and surgical care, especially regarding hospitalization (Rosenstein and Millazzo-Sayre 1981).

In more recent years, legislators have begun to look at the possibility of increasing mental health coverage to the point of parity with general health care. The Federal Mental Health Parity Act of 1996 was a landmark (although limited) federal effort in this direction. It launched a process that continues to this day as state and federal legislators wrestle with how to conceptualize and implement mental health parity. The Mental Health Parity Act of 1996 prohibits different dollar limits for mental health services and general health care. However, it does not stipulate whether insurers must provide mental health coverage, nor does it set the terms and conditions of mental health coverage. Issues such as cost sharing, deductibles, and service limits are not addressed. Also, though the law requires coverage for mental illnesses, it excludes substance abuse, which is often also present in the life of the person struggling with serious mental illness. Further, the federal law exempts health plans purchased directly through the individual market, businesses with fifty or fewer employees, and any business that can demonstrate that parity would result in a cost increase of more than 1 percent. It also does not apply to Medicare/Medicaid coverage. Clearly this was a step in the right direction, but only a small step.

Since that time over thirty states have passed their own versions of mental health party laws, with varying levels of coverage and with varying definitions of mental illnesses to be covered. The most generous ones mandate that mental health benefits be included in all group plans and require parity in all respects—dollar limits, service limits, and cost sharing. The most generous also require coverage for all 297 diagnoses of mental illness as listed in the *DSM-IV*—a point of some controversy.

Extent of Coverage

The question of which mental health diagnoses should be covered is the subject of vigorous debate. Should equal coverage be offered for all mental disorders, or only those that are most serious and debilitating? Many mental health advocates feel that to deny coverage for any disorder, regardless of severity, is simply inexcusable. After all, they point out, medical insurance doesn't keep someone from seeing a doctor for minor needs such as a splinter in the finger or a cold. They argue that any parity legislation should therefore apply to all 297 disorders listed in the *DSM-IV.*

This would provide coverage for tens of millions of people who have any diagnosable mental disorder. Research has shown that 26.2 percent of American adults, about one in four, would meet the *DSM-IV* criteria for a mental disorder in any given year (Kessler, Berglund, et al. 2005). This translates to about 57.7 million adults—a formidable number that does not even include children and adolescents in need of mental health care. Some of these individuals indeed suffer from debilitating mental disorders and are desperately in need of services, but others are experiencing mild emotional difficulties that create little or no disruption in their daily life.

Do all mental disorders equally warrant treatment, are all equally burdensome, or should there be differentiation by severity? As we saw in chapter 1, there is a big difference between a mild mental disorder such as caffeine intoxication and a serious disorder such as major depression— yet both are included in the *DSM-IV.* Caffeine intoxication is an unfortunate consequence of drinking too much coffee but can be easily remedied. On the other hand, major depression can literally kill the one who suffers from it, through suicide. For these reasons, we discussed earlier the need for prioritizing coverage on serious mental illnesses—those that are most burdensome and disruptive in the life of the patient. The following six categories were put forward as a working definition of serious mental illness:

1. Psychotic disorders (e.g., schizophrenia)
2. Mood disorders (e.g., major depression, bipolar disorder)
3. Anxiety disorders (e.g., panic disorder)
4. Childhood disorders (e.g., attention deficit/hyperactivity disorder)
5. Eating disorders (e.g., anorexia)
6. Substance-related disorders (e.g., alcohol dependence)

Research has shown that 6 percent of the adult population suffers from serious mental illness, which translates to about thirteen million people, not including children and adolescents (Kessler, Berglund, et al. 2005). It is these who are most in need of care and thus most in need of parity coverage.

As we have seen, the definition of serious mental illness is based not only on the category of *DSM-IV* diagnosis but also on the extent to which the illness is causing dysfunction in the life of the patient. One of the hallmarks of serious mental illness is that it significantly disrupts life in a way that simply cannot be overcome through effort alone. Disruption might involve weeping uncontrollably throughout the day (major depression), experiencing "heart-stopping" moments of panic (panic attack), or hearing horribly accusatory voices (schizophrenia). When the emotional disorder is severe and the level of dysfunction it causes is significant, that constitutes serious mental illness.

I am sympathetic with those who want to provide coverage for any possible mental illness, which is a compassionate perspective to have. But given the political and economic realities within which reform must take place, and given the pressing need to provide help now for those with serious mental illness, I must agree with those who hold that parity laws should prioritize coverage for serious mental illness.

State-Legislated Mental Health Parity

Over thirty states have mental health parity laws on the books, but the terms of these laws vary greatly. Vermont's parity law, for instance, is one of the oldest in the nation and offers coverage for all *DSM-IV* diagnostic categories. On the other hand, Ohio's parity law, passed more recently, provides coverage only for serious mental illness. Following is a comparison of the two.

Vermont implemented the nation's most comprehensive mental health parity law in 1998, extending equality of health insurance coverage to both mental health and substance abuse needs. All *DSM-IV* diagnostic categories were included. SAMHSA, one of America's two federal mental health agencies, helped commission an evaluation on the impact of this parity law after the first three years (Rosenbach et al. 2003). The analysis focused on how implementation of parity affected the major stakeholders: consumers, providers, health plans, and employers. It carefully analyzed data from the two primary health plans in the state: Kaiser/Community Health Plan and Blue Cross/Blue Shield of Vermont. Together, these plans covered nearly 80 percent of the privately insured population at time of parity implementation. Here are some of the findings of the study:

- Access to mental health outpatient services improved with parity. Both the overall use of outpatient services and the average number of visits per user increased. In other words, parity improved both access to and intensity of mental health outpatient care.
- Consumers paid a smaller share of total spending for covered treatment after parity. Before parity consumers shouldered 30 percent of all costs, but afterwards only 17 percent. The study notes that this probably explains the first point, that people sought out more mental health services and used them longer than they would have before parity.
- Parity did not cause employers to drop coverage and did not significantly raise insurance costs. Only 0.3 percent of Vermont employers reported dropping insurance coverage in response to parity. Health plan spending for mental health services increased for some insurers and decreased for others, but overall there was no dramatic rise in costs.
- Managed care was a key factor in controlling costs. Prior approval, utilization review, and adherence to medical-necessity criteria controlled mental health care costs, despite the increased use of outpatient services. Additionally, providers were required to set treatment goals and document progress before gaining approval for additional sessions.

The Vermont experience demonstrates that it is possible to implement parity without incurring unreasonable costs *if* mental health services are administered within the framework of a managed care environment. Of course, there are many examples of managed care poorly applied, which at its worst can end up denying care to those in need. But managed care itself is simply a tool for controlling health care cost—a tool that can be used either well or poorly. If appropriately applied, managed care strategies can contain cost increases while providing well for those in need.

Vermont required providers to set treatment goals and document progress. This is a step in the right direction, for it focuses on the actual clinical outcomes of mental health care in the life of the patient. Setting clear treatment goals and regularly documenting progress should become standard operating procedure for mental health providers. Doing so not only provides insurers with the data they need to manage care but also invariably leads to improvement in the quality of care. As we saw in chapter 2, that which is measured improves.

Ohio signed their parity law into effect in 2006,[1] and it is too early to analyze the full impact of its implementation. Ohio policy makers chose to apply coverage not to all *DSM-IV* categories of mental disorders but only to "biologically based mental illnesses," defined as

- Schizophrenia
- Schizoaffective disorder
- Major depressive disorder
- Bipolar disorder
- Paranoia and other psychotic disorders
- Obsessive-compulsive disorder
- Panic disorder

The law states that "every group policy of sickness and accident insurance and every [employer self-insurance] plan of health coverage must provide benefits for the diagnosis and treatment of biologically based mental illnesses on the same terms and conditions as, with benefits no less extensive than, those provided under the policy or plan for the diagnosis and treatment of all other physical diseases and disorders." This equal-benefits mandate applies to "coverage of inpatient hospital services, outpatient services, and medication; maximum lifetime benefits; copayments; and individual and family deductibles."[2]

This is a clear and comprehensive statement of what parity is all about—ensuring that persons with mental health needs don't get shortchanged in comparison with those who have medical/surgical needs. This kind of precise language is a good example of what legislators must use when drafting parity legislation. For it is inevitable that any unintended loopholes will be exploited by third-party payers.

Ohio's seven categories of "biologically based mental illness" would be covered under my definition for serious mental illness, since all seven would be included under the categories of psychotic disorders, mood disorders, and anxiety disorders. However, Ohio's parity law leaves out the other three categories of serious mental illness defined in this book: childhood disorders, eating disorders, and substance-related disorders. Childhood and eating disorders should be included because they are widespread and can place heavy burdens on those experiencing them, as well as on their families. Substance-related disorders should be included because many people who struggle with serious mental illness also struggle with substance use (known as "comorbidity" or "dual diagnosis"). To address one without the other is to court relapse.

Vermont's definition of covered mental illnesses is too broad, since it includes all diagnoses listed in the *DSM-IV*. Ohio's definition is too narrow, since it leaves out several major categories of serious mental illness. The challenge is to find a reasonable balance between the two extremes, adequately covering the most pressing needs without opening the door to the "moral hazard" that could result from offering coverage for all 297 mental disorders. The definition of serious mental illness put forward in this book is an attempt to find middle ground between those extremes.

It is important to state that there is room for discussion as to which disorders should or should not be included in the category of covered serious mental illnesses and whether to include substance use disorders. Reasonable people can disagree on exactly where those lines should be drawn. The definition put forward in this book is based on the current literature, on several decades of experience as a provider, and on my experiences as mental health commissioner, but it is not sacrosanct. Perhaps it makes good sense for different states to implement somewhat different definitions based on the particular desires of each state's stakeholders. Then, over time, we can evaluate which definitional approach seems to work the best—to be as broad as possible while still economically feasible. It is better to move ahead with an imperfect definition of serious mental illness than to endlessly debate which diagnoses to cover or to demand that all diagnoses be covered. A wise person once said that if we demand all or nothing, we usually end up with nothing. As states wrestle with parity legislation, let us leave room for variation and innovation in the confidence that the relative advantages and disadvantages of different approaches will become clear over time (so long as we are measuring outcomes). We will then be able to fine-tune the best legislative parameters for mental health parity.

Federal Mental Health Parity Legislation

Out of growing concerns for the lack of coverage for persons with serious mental illness, the federal government began addressing mental health parity in the 1990s and in 1996 passed the Mental Health Parity Act. As noted above, this was a symbolically important but functionally limited effort to begin closing the gap between coverage for mental health needs and coverage for medical/surgical care. At that time only five states had legislation requiring any form of mental health parity in private-sector health insurance coverage. Over the next four years, over thirty states passed laws mandating mental health coverage. This was done in part to avoid federal regulatory oversight by passing laws that would be comparable to the federal parity law. But it was also simply a result of the federal government having put the issue of parity on the nation's agenda as an important public policy matter to be reckoned with. It is clear that federal action often leads to state action, even if indirectly. Congress serves as a bully pulpit for all areas of public policy, including mental health care coverage.

As we have seen, the states' parity laws are highly variable in their definition of covered mental illnesses and in the extent to which full parity is actually accomplished. Even more importantly, they are limited in application by the federal Employee Retirement Income Security Act of 1974 (ERISA), which preempts state regulations applying to "self-insured" employer health plans (Harrison 2002). Over 130 million Americans have employer-sponsored health insurance, and over half of these are covered through self-insured plans that are exempted from state regulation per ERISA. Thus these health plans are not at all affected by the current state-level mental health parity laws and would be subject only to new federal parity legislation. For these reasons (among others), Congress has worked for the past ten years to try to expand the original 1996 Mental Health Parity Act so as to achieve full parity coverage with medical/surgical benefits.

These efforts recently paid off. The Paul Wellstone and Pete Domenici Mental Health Parity and Addiction Equity Act of 2008 was signed into law by President Bush on October 3, 2008.[3]

The mental health parity bill was supported by both parties and by both the legislative branch (Congress) and the executive branch (the president). All agreed that it makes good sense to correct the ERISA exemption and advance mental health parity coverage. Nonetheless, passage of this legislation was difficult primarily because of two critical concerns— extent of coverage and costs entailed. Should parity apply to all mental illness and substance use disorders or only to those that are most serious? Who should pay for the costs of parity coverage—the government? The private sector? Either way—how?

Regarding extent of coverage, as noted above, mental health advocates have lobbied for any parity legislation to be based on the *DSM-IV* and to include coverage for all its 297 diagnoses. However, third-party payers argued successfully that the *DSM-IV* should not be included in the bill, lest insurers end up paying for diagnoses such as caffeine intoxication and jet lag. Consequently, references to the *DSM-IV* were dropped, and accordingly the bill does not stipulate which mental illnesses must be covered. The result? It is more likely that "parity" coverage will be extended on a priority basis to those with serious mental illness, which seems to make good sense. Coverage for lesser needs may end up being an option for purchase above and beyond "parity-level" coverage. In other words, if a person prefers full coverage for all 297 categories of mental illness, that option should be available but at a higher cost.

What about cost? There have been conflicting estimates of the actual cost of implementing full mental health parity coverage—from insignificant to monumental. The 2008 Wellstone-Domenici Mental Health Parity Act addressed this matter by putting in several fiscal safety nets for the third-party payer. Like the 1996 law, this one applies only to employers with fifty or more employees. Also, if mental health parity costs an insurer more than a 2 percent increase in benefits (1 percent after the first year), then the insurer may claim exemption for one year. If this occurs, the insurer may be audited to determine the reason for the cost increase, with the goal being to implement parity the following year in a more fiscally manageable manner. Further, the bill calls for the Government Accountability Office to study parity-related rates and coverage issues and to report to Congress within three years to make sure that the intent of the legislation is indeed carried out and that the cost is reasonable.

The new parity law becomes effective on January 1, 2010, and thankfully will apply to the millions of individuals in self-funded plans who were exempt from the 1996 parity law because of ERISA. Also, whereas the 1996 law established parity only for annual and lifetime dollar limits, the 2008 law applies to all financial and treatment limitations. This includes deductibles, copayments, coinsurance, out-of-pocket expenses, number of days of inpatient coverage, frequency of treatment, and total number of visits. What does all this mean? If implemented effectively, this law may finally do away with the undue financial burdens currently borne by insured families and individuals struggling with serious mental illness.

What about choice of provider? The 2008 parity law stipulates that any group health plan that provides out-of-network access for medical/surgical benefits must provide equal access for mental health and substance use disorders. This is a critical point, as many consumers have experienced the acute dilemma of either working with a less-than-ideal mental health provider who is on their limited preferred provider list or paying out of pocket. If this provision is implemented effectively, it will significantly broaden the provider choices currently available to insured mental health consumers.

In sum, the 2008 mental health parity law has the potential to be a great step toward providing parity coverage for serious mental illness. However, as is often said, "The devil is in the details," and this law has yet to be implemented. It is critical that both federal and state level policy makers work carefully to implement this law in a manner that will accomplish the intended goal—making it easier for those with serious mental illness to get the care they need for recovery. It is also critical that new funds available through parity are not used to simply grow the status quo mental health system, since it's broken. Instead, funds should be used to advance mental health reform by requiring the use of evidence-based practices and outcome data, as discussed in chapter 2.

The Critical Issue of Medical Necessity

Gaining parity coverage for serious mental illness is a huge step forward in providing for persons struggling with these debilitating disorders. It is just not fair for insurers to discriminate against emotional disorders, thus ensuring that whoever has one will have to shoulder not only the burden of the mental illness but also the added burden of poor coverage. But parity alone won't necessarily change much unless another issue is resolved at the same time—the issue of medical necessity (e.g., see Sabin and Daniels 1994).

Dr. William Ford, a mental health policy specialist, has addressed the topic of medical necessity as applied to mental health (Ford 1998). He noted that medical necessity results from the fact that all health care service delivery systems assume coverage will only be offered for those services that are truly necessary to treat the illness. After all, providing unnecessary services increases the overall cost of health care, thus squandering limited resources that could be made available for others who need them. So, for example, plastic surgery may be desired by patients dissatisfied with their nose, but this would not constitute a medically necessary treatment for illness. Consequently, insurers must develop a definition of medical necessity—what is required to qualify for coverage. In the realm of physical health care, a common definition would stipulate that services provided must be

- For the treatment of a diagnosable illness
- Consistent with generally accepted medical practice
- Efficient, in the use of less expensive but equally effective treatments
- Not for the patient's or provider's convenience

This definition makes sense for medical/surgical needs but not for mental health services, though most insurers apply it (or something close) to both. The trouble is that in the realm of mental health care this definition is intrinsically shortsighted. It provides for services when a patient is floridly experiencing the symptoms of mental illness, which is a good starting point. But what about prevention of relapse? What about making sure a mild disorder doesn't develop into a more serious one? What about doing what it takes so that the patient can function well in his or her home community? Consider the case of Carol.

"CAROL"
Carol was a middle-aged woman who had worked many years in cafeteria services for the local school system. Although her pay was not what she wanted it to be, she thought she had good health benefits—the same as anyone else in the school system. She had a devoted husband, two grown children who were starting their own families, many close friends, and plenty of enjoyable activities. To her surprise, she found herself experiencing a major clinical depression (including weeping frequently, not eating, and barely

sleeping) on a cyclical basis—usually in the dead of winter. For several years she attempted to simply "tough it out" by pushing ahead with life anyway. Usually after about three months the depression would lift.

But one year the depression became more severe than ever, and Carol tried to end her life by swallowing a bottle of sleeping pills. After a trip to the emergency room, where her stomach was pumped and she was screened for mental illness, she was admitted to a psychiatric hospital with the diagnosis of acute major depression with suicidal ideation (thoughts). Her insurance covered inpatient care up to a limit of fourteen days per year so long as the criteria for medical necessity was met, which in this case meant experiencing depression and having suicidal thoughts. Carol responded well to the hospital's antidepressant medications, her mood brightened, her suicidal thoughts receded, and she was discharged. It seemed that all was well, until she came back the following winter in the same state—depressed and with suicidal tendencies. Once again she was stabilized on medications, and once again she was discharged.

The following fall she began searching for other options and called on a psychiatrist who specialized in treating depression in women, asking for help before the "winter blues" hit. Since she was not experiencing the symptoms of depression, she had to pay out of pocket for treatment. Through a series of diagnostic tests, it was determined that Carol could in fact be suffering from "seasonal affective disorder"—meaning that the lack of sunshine in winter triggered her depression. So the psychiatrist tried a different approach. She had Carol start using a special lamp designed to make up for the lack of sunshine in winter, and in so doing found that Carol's depression was averted. All that she needed was light! In subsequent years, Carol continued to use the special lamp as needed and had no more troubles with winter depressions.

Why wasn't this determined earlier? Because as soon as Carol no longer met the criteria of "medical necessity" for treatment she was discharged to the usual minimal outpatient follow-up (monthly checkup on medications). Her insurance company had no intention of putting extra time and effort, such as expensive diagnostic services, into a patient who was symptom free for the moment. Even if they agreed there was a high risk of expensive relapse the following year if nothing further was done, they still would not necessarily be motivated to provide additional care. After all, she might well be insured by another carrier by that time, in which case prevention services would only benefit a rival provider! A new definition of medical necessity is needed for mental health services, one that takes into account the need for a long-term, preventive approach to care. It cannot be based on diagnostic status alone. It must take into account other variables.

The solution is to focus not just on the diagnostic classification but also on level of functioning over time. The goal of treatment for someone suffering from serious mental illness must be for them to do well in the long run, not just recover symptomatically for a brief period. This is consistent with the "recovery" model that seeks to provide whatever it takes for a patient to succeed in the home community. It is the ethical thing to do, and it is also the economically efficient thing to do. Think how much money Carol's insurance company would have saved if they had put more resources into diagnosing her disorder and treating it preventatively before it next occurred. A lamp costs a lot less than a stay in the hospital!

So perhaps in the realm of mental health what is needed is not so much a definition of medical necessity as one of "clinical necessity." This could be defined as a set of criteria to determine when a patient with serious mental illness is in need of services. Drawing on Ford's work, I offer the following definition of clinical necessity, on two levels. The words in parentheses shift the definition from "all mental illness" to "serious mental illness," as defined in chapter 1. To qualify for payment, mental health services must be

- For the treatment of (serious) mental illness and substance use disorders, or symptoms of these disorders, and the remediation of (significant) impairments in day-to-day functioning related to them, or
- For the purpose of preventing the need for a more intensive level of mental health and substance abuse care, or
- For the purpose of preventing relapse of persons with (serious) mental illness and substance use disorders, and
- Consistent with evidence-based, generally accepted clinical practice for mental and substance use disorders, and
- Efficient, in the sense of preferring a less expensive but equally effective treatment where possible, and
- Not for the patient's or provider's convenience

The primary difference between medical necessity and clinical necessity is that the first three bullets are "or" phrases. What this means is that treatment can be deemed clinically necessary to treat symptoms, *or* to prevent more serious mental illness, *or* to prevent relapse. In the case of Carol, this would have allowed her to receive diagnostic services and preventive treatment (the lamp) and thus to avoid the cyclical hospitalization into which she fell.

Hospitalization is of course sometimes necessary, as it is the only way to provide a completely controlled and safe environment for people needing that level of security and care. But it should be rare, in that most serious mental illnesses can be treated in the home community with intensive home- and community-based care. To send a mental health patient to the hospital needlessly is to commit two "sins"—one against the person and the other economic. The "personal sin" is to lock a patient away against his or her will for a period of time, knowing that it is likely to harm the patient's self-concept and damage self-confidence. The patient may well come out of the hospital less motivated to take responsibility for his or her own mental health care. The "economic sin" is to waste funds that could better be used elsewhere to provide care that is critically needed.

With the current concept of medical necessity it is difficult to take a long-term view of treatment needs, whether or not symptoms are present. This is particularly so for long-term conditions that may be in remission, such as Carol's seasonal affective disorder, but for which ongoing treatment is necessary to avoid more intensive levels of care in the future. Clinical necessity would correct the many shortcomings of medical necessity as applied to mental health care. Clinical necessity has the critical advantage of supporting relapse prevention, as well as providing services to prevent a later need for higher levels of care. Clinical necessity, combined with parity coverage for serious mental illness, would make it much easier for managed mental health care to lead to the patient's recovery.

Denial of Care versus Overdiagnosis

Medical necessity rigidly applied to mental health services is problematic in other ways as well. For instance, reimbursement parameters can improperly affect the determination of medical necessity for a given service by a provider, leading to either denial of care or overdiagnosis.

If a provider's income is reduced by increased utilization, as in a capitated system of care, a subtle incentive exists for the provider to deny care. A capitated system is one in which the provider is paid a set annual fee for each person covered, regardless of treatment required, which means that more profit results from less treatment. In such a setting, the diagnosis of a person suffering from an anxiety disorder may be minimized by the mental health provider, and the patient described to the insurer as simply managing a typical life problem. Thus the diagnostic criteria for medical necessity are not met, and less money is spent on provision of services. The same incentive to deny care applies to the insurer as well, whose self-interest may subtly influence the case-by-case application of the concept of medical necessity.

On the other hand, if a provider's income is enhanced by increasing service utilization, as in a fee-for-service system (the more service provided the more revenue received), then a subtle incentive exists for the provider to overdiagnose or overrepresent symptoms to public or private insurers. For instance, a client struggling with a typical life problem such as career challenges may be classified as suffering from major depression so that clinical treatment can be funded, when vocational counseling would have perhaps better suited the need.

Either way, the patient is not well served. The "diagnosis only"–based approach to determining medical necessity can easily be tainted by nonclinical factors and can thereby hinder the provision of appropriate care. The use of the more flexible concept of clinical necessity, which recognizes not only diagnosis but also the need for preventive care, makes it easier for the provider to meet the actual needs of the patient. Clinical necessity also incorporates a greater focus on the patient's level of functioning, since it includes the remediation of dysfunction related to the mental illness. The assessment and tracking of daily functioning helps avoid both denial of care and overdiagnosis, since it measures clinical outcome on the basis of how well the patient is actually doing. It is difficult to overdiagnose a patient who is functioning well, and it is difficult to deny care for a patient who is highly dysfunctional.

But what about preventive care—how does that work? In its zeal to avoid moral hazard and overdiagnosis, might not a third-party payer simply refuse any care not fully required by the patient's current symptoms? A strict adherence to medical necessity could easily do so. But with the concept of clinical necessity a longer-term view is required, one that includes prevention of relapse and worse problems down the road. It recognizes that strict medical necessity, applied to mental health care, often has unanticipated negative cost consequences. For example, to deny outpatient psychotherapy as not medically necessary for a person who is depressed because of marital problems is actually shortsighted if that person later decompensates for lack of treatment and is hospitalized for major depression. So it becomes important to assess for long-term needs so that long-term costs may be minimized. In some cases, the third-party payer might actually end up encouraging higher use of outpatient services, particularly for patients likely to relapse or for those who without such services would require more intensive levels of care.

The most challenging cases are those who, like Carol, need continuing treatment even when there are no symptoms at all of a mental or substance use disorder. This is particularly true for long-term conditions such as bipolar disorder or substance abuse that may be in remission, but for which ongoing treatment is necessary to avoid more intensive levels of care in the future. Within the constrictions of medical necessity, it is very difficult to draw any conclusion other than to deny care. But with clinical necessity both the provider and the insurer are motivated to take a long-term view and provide preventive services. This not only holds down costs in the long run but makes it more likely that the patient will be given what he or she needs to succeed in the home community.[4] Thus everyone wins—the patient, the community, and the insurer.

Even with parity coverage for mental illness now beginning, access to treatment is still limited by the current definition of medical necessity. A new approach, called clinical necessity, is needed for determining when treatment is required for mental health and substance abuse problems. Clinical necessity will help to address the shortcoming of the current concept of medical necessity while avoiding the misuse of benefits. The risk of moral hazard is contained by an assessment-based focus on long-term needs that goes beyond simple diagnosis. The concept also has the advantage of supporting relapse prevention, as well as providing services to prevent the need for higher levels of care later on. Clinical necessity, combined with mental health parity, would go a long way to improving the quality of mental health care and the likelihood of recovery.

The Uninsured

This all sounds well and good for people who are either covered by private health insurance or eligible for state and/or federal funds. But what about those who are not insured at all, and not eligible? What about the forty-seven million Americans who by choice or necessity have no access to either private or public funds? They will not be helped by the best parity laws in the land, either federal or state. Their plight weighs heavily on the nation, as indeed it should. America is one of the last advanced industrialized countries to solve the challenge of how to provide health care for all citizens.

There are many ways to join the ranks of the uninsured. One way is to have an expensive illness paid for by an insurance company that then proceeds to drop coverage. Another way is to lose one's job, or to work for an employer who does not offer benefits. Another way is to have "preexisting conditions" that make coverage either unaffordable or unattainable. Regardless of how one gets there, people without insurance are very much at the mercy of a broken mental health system. They tend not to seek care until it is urgent and then end up in emergency rooms—or jail. The mental health services received may or may not be appropriate and effective, but there is no option other than to take whatever is offered. As we have seen, even with insurance and financial resources serious mental illness is very difficult to manage. Without insurance, without resources, it is a thousand times worse.

The irony is that society often ends up paying more for a person without insurance than timely treatment would have cost in the first place. This is because it is usually less expensive to treat mental illness in its early stages (e.g., mild depression or occasional alcohol abuse) than it is to treat it when it's out of control (e.g., major depression with suicide attempts or alcohol dependency). But without coverage, people with serious mental illness are not likely to receive care until their needs are great—typically not until they have become a threat to themselves or to others. Thus it is as if society were saying to the uninsured: "Sorry, you are not welcome to treatment until you are in a really bad state. Please come back when you are, and we will then provide you with expensive (but not necessarily effective) care for the shortest duration possible." This has sometimes tragic consequences in the lives of people who are uninsured, is financially costly, and in the final analysis makes no sense. Why not figure out a reasonable way to provide health care coverage for all?

The question of whether to provide universal health and mental health care coverage is currently being deliberated at both federal and state levels, and some states are experimenting with new approaches. It is hopefully just a matter of time until the nation moves toward some form of universal coverage, although partisan bickering may delay that time. It is beyond the scope of this book to explore the advantages and disadvantages of the various potential universal health care strategies. Should coverage be mandatory, or should it be optional for the benefit of the young and healthy who might prefer not to spend money on health insurance? Should coverage be funded through a single-payer system such as a government agency, or should it consist of subsidies so that people can afford to purchase private policies? How can universal coverage be offered in a way that does not lower the quality of health care and yet does not break the bank?

There are no easy answers to these questions, but a nation that can send a man to the moon can surely find an innovative way to provide health care for all Americans. State and federal legislators simply must put partisan rancor aside, roll up their sleeves, and solve this problem for the sake of their constituents who suffer the burden of uninsured medical needs. Mental health advocacy organizations should join others in encouraging voters to support only those candidates who follow through on this matter.

Two comments can be made from the perspective of a transformed mental health care system. First, unless the problem of the uninsured is solved mental health reform can succeed only in part. Universal coverage would mean that anyone with serious mental illness could receive the treatment they need and avoid ending up at emergency rooms, in prison, or on the street. Otherwise, a large number will not have the care they need regardless of parity and other reforms and will continue to live out the tragedy of serious mental illness untreated. Second, if the health and mental health care systems are reformed, then some streams of funding will become available to help cover the costs of universal health care. For instance, many hospitals currently receive significant yearly funding called "disproportionate share" that is intended to reimburse their cost of care for uninsured patients. Such funds would of course no longer be needed if there were no uninsured patients, and the money could instead go toward helping to cover the cost of universal coverage.

It is critical that the matter of mental health transformation not be framed as related to one particular party or one position on the political spectrum. Liberals and conservatives, Democrats and Republicans, all are capable of experiencing mental disorders—and need coverage. Most have seen friends or family members struggle to cope with a mental illness. Hopefully the differences between the parties have to do only with how we achieve universal or near-universal coverage—not whether to do so. If so, then what is needed is an honest and informative national dialogue on the topic, leading to a good faith effort to insure all or most of the forty-seven million who have been left out of America's health care system.

It is time for America to address the problem of so many citizens living without the benefits of health insurance. It may not be a basic human right, but reasonable coverage for all makes sense on many levels, both ethically and economically. More to the point of this book, it provides a scenario within which mental health care reform can proceed for all citizens rather than a select few. Universal coverage advances the cause of reforming the health and mental health care systems. Hopefully the fact that it is under serious consideration by the current administration is another signal that a tipping point for real reform is about to be reached.

Conclusion

Many voices in America are calling for mental health reform or system transformation or are simply demanding that the broken mental health care system be fixed. Mine is one of those voices. Too many people are struggling with serious mental illness and not receiving the care they need to be able to live successfully in their home community. Too many billions of dollars are being spent on services that are not particularly effective. There is too much discrimination against mental health care on the part of public- and private-sector insurers. This chapter has presented the case for carefully implementing parity coverage for mental health care, together with redefining the concept of medical necessity into clinical necessity. Were both to be done, significant new funding would become available from insurers for treating serious mental illness.

However, it would be tragic if increased funding served simply as a means to expand the status quo. The status quo is broken! Therefore, whatever steps are taken to reform mental health services must be carefully implemented so as not to simply throw more money at the current failed system of care. Policy makers must be committed to developing something new—an outcome-oriented, community-based system of mental health care—one that welcomes innovation, is not afraid of accountability, and promotes recovery. Only then will we achieve the high quality of care and positive clinical outcomes that patients and their families deserve and demand. For this to happen, parity and clinical necessity as defined in this chapter must be combined with the critical concepts we discussed earlier, specifically:

- Focus first on serious mental illness so that those who most need care receive it on a priority basis.
- Use clinical outcome data and evidence-based practices to ensure high quality of care.
- Establish a competitive and fair managed health care environment so that consumers have choices and so that funding is not wasted.

The policy recommendations from the first four chapters are not meant to stand alone. They work together in a complementary manner and taken together would significantly transform the current broken mental health system of care. There is a tendency among policy makers to pick and choose among possible legislative alternatives, looking for the "low-hanging fruit" of easy issues that will generate acclaim and little resistance. Unfortunately, mental health care reform is not in that category of issues. Visionary and courageous leadership will be required on the part of policy makers for reform to occur. Such leadership is rare but not impossible to find, as will be explored in chapter 6.

These four factors are critical, but one more is also essential—a new role for mental health service consumers and their families. Gone are the days when consumers blindly accepted whatever the treating authorities recommended without so much as a discussion of the options. Mental health patients, indeed all patients, are demanding to be included in their provider's decision-making process since the outcome so powerfully affects their lives. They are also demanding to be at the policy table to have some input into mental health policies that will shape whatever care is made available. This is healthy, and another key component for transforming the mental health system of care, as will be shown in the next chapter.

5

Let the People Speak

In Australia, Canada, Europe, New Zealand, the USA and elsewhere the mental health advocacy movement is burgeoning . . . [and] . . . has led to major changes in the way persons with mental disorders are regarded. Consumers have begun to articulate their own vision of the services they need and want. They are also making increasingly informed decisions about treatment and other matters affecting their daily life.

World Health Organization,
Advocacy for Mental Health (2003)

Nearly every consumer of mental health services who testified before or submitted comments to the Commission expressed the need to fully participate in his or her recovery plan. . . . Consumers and families told the Commission that having hope and the opportunity to regain control of their lives was vital to their recovery.

The President's New Freedom Commission on
Mental Health, *Achieving the Promise* (2003)

AT THE CORE of the American democratic concept is the principle that everyone affected by a policy or decision should have a voice at the table. This principle is based on the belief that people can be trusted to make good decisions on their own behalf. In America there is no place for autocracy, whether in government or in health care. Yet currently, a great many people with mental illness feel disenfranchised and disempowered by the way they are treated when seeking care.[1] They and their families are shuffled from one provider to another and told what to do, without being able to participate in the clinical decision-making process. Further, they are typically left out of policy and program deliberations. They are often not at the table when new programs are being contemplated, when policies are being drafted, or when treatments are being evaluated for effectiveness. Instead, consumers and family members alike tend to be brushed off and told that the experts must decide these matters. However, as we have seen, "the times they are a-changing" in that persons with mental illness are demanding to have more say in policy and treatment decisions that affect their lives. This is healthy, and one more sign that the mental health care system is on the verge of real transformation (Kelly 2003b). It is shifting from an autocratic model of mental health care based on simply following the doctor's orders to one that is more participatory, more democratic, and as a result much more effective.

"ALISON"

Alison was a hardworking and promising college junior when she first experienced severe depression. Not knowing what was wrong other than the fact that she cried often and wasn't eating or sleeping well, she went to the student health clinic. Her first encounter with the clinic MD was not particularly helpful. After taking her history, the MD concluded that her sad feelings were primarily driven by working too hard on her academics. She was simply overworked, the doctor suggested, and needed to take a break—to get out more in order to feel better. He prescribed sleeping pills and a brief time off from studies and sent her on her way. Alison dutifully followed the doctor's orders but found no relief. Unfortunately, she went from bad to worse and was back in the clinic a month later, this time talking about hurting herself. Her sense of hopelessness had grown, and she was considering the possibility of suicide as a final way out. The threat of self-harm got her quickly to the on-duty psychologist, who correctly diagnosed major depression with suicidal thoughts. The prescribed treatment involved antidepressant medication to supplement the sleeping pills, as well as antianxiety medication to address Alison's worried feelings that burdened her.[2] Also, Alison was to have therapy weekly with the student health services psychologist until her depression lifted.

Alison dutifully complied, even though she felt "overmedicated" from the prescriptions. She felt groggy in the mornings and lacked her usual mental focus throughout the day. Her sad mood lifted a little, and she stopped having thoughts about hurting herself, but she still did not feel well. She was gaining weight from the medications, and her therapy sessions did not seem to help. The psychologist, who had recently completed specialized training in the psychoanalytic tradition, concluded that Alison was suffering from denial of her own sexuality.[3] Accordingly, much of the discussion focused on Alison's dating life and her unmet needs for intimacy. Although Alison agreed that she was somewhat lonely and indeed wished she could find the right partner, she felt strongly that this was not what was driving her depression. She asked the psychologist if they could work on other matters, such as her tendency to always put herself down, but the request was interpreted as "resistance."[4] She also asked to cut back on the prescribed medications but was advised against it for the time being.

Finally, in an act of desperation, Alison decided to seek out a new mental health provider and ended up working with a psychiatrist across town—a woman who had an excellent reputation for treating depression in women. It was financially difficult for Alison to seek alternative care, since her student insurance did not cover off-campus providers, but she was determined to find someone with whom she felt she could work collaboratively. The psychiatrist invited her to carefully evaluate whether this was the approach to treatment Alison was looking for, which she did—asking many good questions. After that, Alison decided to continue under the psychiatrist's care.

Over the next several weeks, as they worked together to help Alison overcome her depression in ways that made sense to her, it became clear that her judgment was correct. She did not need to be on three medications, and she improved somewhat as the psychiatrist began tapering her off the sleeping pills and antianxiety medication. Alison continued on the antidepressant medication for a few more months, then tapered off that as well. She was also correct that her depression was not driven primarily by loneliness or intimacy issues. Her main need was to understand and overcome a tendency to put herself down with automatic thoughts such as "I'm stupid, I'm just a loser, just like my dad always said." Such thoughts (and the associated negative feelings) were hindering her academic progress, robbing her of any sense of joy, and creating a needlessly negative self-image. As Alison began to replace the negative thoughts with more accurate concepts (e.g., "I may not be a genius, but my grades show I have what it takes to do well here"), the depression lost its grip and she began to recover her positive spirit. After about three months of cognitive psychotherapy, her depression was a thing of the past and she had learned how to better manage future depressive tendencies whenever they might arise.

What went wrong in the college health clinic? In a word, the clinic doctors did not listen to their patient. They assumed they knew best what she needed and prescribed treatment accordingly, despite her consistent feedback to the contrary. Had they used a tracking survey to measure the extent to which their patients were improving and satisfied with treatment, they would have found out early on that Alison was not responding well and needed something other than what was being offered. Most persons struggling with serious mental illness actually have a lot to say about how they are doing and what sort of treatment they would prefer, either on surveys or simply in dialogue with their provider. They are fully capable of grasping the differences between various treatment modalities and would love to be able to weigh in on the clinical decisions being made on their behalf. So why doesn't that happen?

Old School versus New School

The medical profession, and by extension the mental health profession, has historically viewed the patient as a passive recipient of needed care and the doctor as the expert who knows what treatment to provide ("doctor knows best"). For most of us, this perspective is strengthened each time we visit the family doctor. We are shuffled in and told to change our clothes for a small paper robe that leaves us feeling cold, silly-looking, and vulnerable. This contrasts with the doctor's formal white lab coat, which contributes to a power differential between doctor and patient. The doctor is knowledgeable and in control. The patient is vulnerable and in need of help. With no time to spare, most doctors are not interested in discussing treatment options or explaining how each would work. They may tolerate a few questions, but mostly they want to finish the exam, prescribe treatment, and move on to the next patient urgently awaiting their professional attention. As a result, most of us have been trained not to question the authority or wisdom of health care professionals. We should be grateful for their help, not question their decisions or waste valuable time.

Research, however, has pointed out an embarrassing fact—that many decisions made by well-meaning but hard-pressed health professionals are in fact erroneous (e.g., Kohn, Corrigan, and Donaldson 2000). It is not that doctors are careless but simply that they are not perfect. Consequently there has been a rising chorus of voices calling for improvements, including allowing patients to have greater input into their own health care decisions (e.g., Langewitz, Nübling, and Weber 2006). The same can of course be said for mental health care providers. Psychologists, psychiatrists, social workers, and others are trying to provide what will best fit their patients' needs. But nobody is perfect. Therefore it is actually in everyone's best interest for the mental health professional to engage the patient in meaningful dialogue about treatment options before prescribing care. It also makes good sense to invite regular feedback from patients as to how well they're doing and how satisfied (or not) they are with treatment.

In my years as a practicing psychologist I (like many other providers) have come to appreciate how important and helpful it is to invite the patient into the decision-making process. Some are not interested and are content to simply accept whatever treatment is recommended, which is fine. But most are quite glad to participate more actively in clinical decisions affecting them and often have excellent ideas that serve to improve the overall quality of care. It sounds so simple, but asking a question such as "How satisfied are you with your treatment so far?" often yields opportunity to fine-tune care and ultimately speed improvement. For instance, such feedback may lead to varying the frequency of sessions on the basis of the patient's preference for more (or less) treatment. Further, it empowers patients to feel more in control of their life, which is a critical point for anyone struggling with a mental illness.

I have found anecdotally that an age or generational factor comes into play regarding collaborative treatment. More elderly persons often prefer a more traditionally autocratic approach and are not as interested in reviewing treatment options or progress. Younger persons, in contrast, often welcome the invitation to collaborate in their own care and have a lot of helpful things to say. This may be strictly age related, or a function of generational differences, or a combination of the two. In any event, many younger patients among those I have seen particularly welcome the "new school" approach of collaborative mental health care. They seem more comfortable seeing themselves as empowered to advocate on their own behalf.

On Mental Health Advocacy

Thankfully, over the past thirty-plus years increasing attention has been given to the needs and rights of persons with serious mental illness. This is in stark contrast with the "lock them away" attitude that prevailed through the 1950s, when hospitalization was practically the only treatment available. Originally the advocacy goal was to reduce stigma associated with mental illness, reduce discrimination, and ensure that the basic human rights of those with mental disorders would be protected. More recently, advocacy organizations have broadened out to offer services to those in need (e.g., family support groups) and to get more directly involved in the political and legal process on behalf of those with mental illness. This is done both on a "class action" level by advocates who work in the legislative arena and on an individual level by advocates who represent and support individuals struggling to find effective care in the mental health system. Some advocacy organizations consist primarily of family members caring for their loved ones with mental illness, whereas others consist of mental health consumers themselves (sometimes called self-advocates).

The various groups differ along many lines, including whether or not to work within the current mental health system structure. Some prefer the term *survivor* to *consumer* because they see their primary challenge as surviving the ineffective and autocratic mental health care system. Such persons, having in many cases been ill served, tend to denounce the current system of care and call for outright avoidance of professional mental health providers. Most advocates I have worked with, however, want to work with mental health policy makers, insurers, and providers to improve the system of care.

Taken together, these various advocacy organizations provide what would otherwise be a missing voice—the voice of persons with serious mental illness. They have lobbied long and hard, and with some success, to gain access to policy and treatment deliberations in both the public and private sectors. But there is a long way to go.

Advocacy is based on the notion of one person speaking on behalf of another, and in the realm of mental health that is particularly appropriate, since persons with active mental illness are often ill equipped to advocate effectively for their own needs. As long as we have a mental health care system that is difficult to navigate and not particularly effective (as indeed the current one too often is), we will need advocates who work on behalf of those caught in the system. For example, nonprofit organizations such as the National Alliance for the Mentally Ill (www.nami.org) and Mental Health America (formerly the National Mental Health Association, www.nmha.org) have worked hard to advocate for the needs of persons with mental illness and their families. They do everything from lobbying legislators to pass needed mental health bills, to providing support services for those struggling with mental illness. Other advocacy organizations focus on a particular mental disorder and offer helpful resources for anyone struggling with that disorder: for example, the Depression and Bipolar Support Alliance (www.dbsalliance.org). These and other mental health advocacy organizations provide extensive outreach and educational services for consumers and family members, with a personal touch that eludes government agencies. They have superb Web sites that can answer just about any question regarding mental illness and how to manage it and can refer the interested party to local support groups.

Advocacy organizations can accomplish a lot but not everything, since ultimately it is up to the individual consumer to demand the quality of care that is needed. After all, the goal is not to perpetuate advocacy organizations per se but to create the kind of mental health system that gives persons with serious mental illness what they need to recover their place in the home community. The top priority, therefore, should be to empower and equip patients and their families to take a more proactive role in the recovery process. This means inviting persons with serious mental illness, and their families, to collaborate in everything from policy making to treatment decisions to service evaluation. In varying degrees, this approach is being tested out in both public- and private-sector settings. Increasingly, state and federal mental health agencies, and private-sector mental health organizations, are beginning to include consumers in policy or program discussions. However, it is not always clear whether the consumer's voice is really being heeded. In some cases, it seems as if consumers are seated at the table only so that the organization can report later that their input was considered. Obviously, the point is not to create an illusion of consumer participation but to welcome genuine input from those most affected by the decisions made. The guiding principle should be that the voice of those who struggle with serious mental illness is heard and heeded by policy makers and providers alike. This takes effort but is well worth it.

As a case in point, during my tenure as Virginia's mental health commissioner, a state legislator sympathetic to mental health needs decided to include an additional $500,000 in the budget so that the Mental Health

Department could pilot-test new services. The department's central office staff was set to distribute this equally to the state's forty community mental health centers, but that would have meant that each would get only a small sum to work with—thus making it unlikely that anything significant could be tested. So I called for a meeting with consumers and other stakeholders to discuss the matter. The consumers present were unanimous in suggesting that all the money be given to one mental health center in order to pilot-test a service Virginia did not yet have, the Program for Assertive Community Treatment [PACT]), which had been shown to be effective in breaking the vicious cycle of hospitalization and discharge for persons with serious mental illness.[5] This was a much better plan, and I agreed. The money was thus given in its entirety to a competitively selected mental health center, which went on to demonstrate that the PACT program indeed worked well. As a result, PACT became a significant and effective part of the services offered by Virginia's Mental Health Department. Had we not paid attention to the voice of the consumers at the table, the funding would probably have been wasted on dozens of small projects.

The World Health Organization (WHO) has been supporting the need for mental health advocacy for many years (World Health Organization 2003). They have encouraged relevant government organizations around the world, such as SAMHSA in the United States and ministries of health in other nations, to dialogue with consumers and advocacy organizations when creating or evaluating mental health policies. WHO notes that in several countries advocacy organizations have become particularly effective in the public policy arena (e.g., NAMI in the United States, ENOSH [the Israeli Non-Profit Mental Health Association] in Israel, Mind [formally the National Association for Mental Health] in Britain). These groups have successfully raised public awareness about mental illness and have acted effectively as "pressure groups" for improvements in services. Consequently, in several countries consumers have begun to articulate their own vision as to the types of services they most need. They have begun asking to be included in the decision-making process that determines their own treatment options.

Having established that mental health advocacy is important, let us consider implications for consumers and their families, mental health providers, and policy makers. But first a question of basic human rights must be addressed.

Commitment: A Question of Human Rights

It is important for all mental health consumers to understand that they have the right to participate to the full extent possible in the selection, provision, and evaluation of services provided on their behalf. Just because a person has a serious mental illness does not mean that he or she must forfeit the basic right to self-determination regarding his or her own care. At the same time, we must recognize that mental illness can so debilitate persons that for a short time they may indeed be incapable of making a rational decision on their own behalf and thus are in a state that can be dangerous both for themselves and for others. This is why all states have "commitment" laws, regulations that stipulate a legal process and clinical assessment procedure for determining whether an individual should be required by the state to be hospitalized for mental health treatment. Generally speaking, commitment to hospitalization (sometimes accompanied with mandatory treatment) is granted when a person struggling with serious mental illness is found to be a threat either to self or to others. This is a sensitive topic, and many consumers understandably have strong feelings about it one way or the other, especially those who have seen such laws misapplied.

It is a challenge to hit the right balance regarding commitment laws, and the stakes are high on either extreme. If the commitment bar is set too low, then a person may be needlessly locked up in a psychiatric hospital when other interventions would have been more effective and appropriate. I ask the reader to consider finding yourself in such a situation, how terrifying it would be to be locked away from society and asked (or even persuaded) to take powerful medications that alter your thoughts and feelings. This loss of the basic right to self-determination could theoretically happen to anyone, since everyone is capable of experiencing mental illness; thus the bar must not be set too low. On the other hand, if the bar is set too high, then a person may fail to receive the care needed and may continue indefinitely in the painful and anguishing symptoms of mental illness. Further, he or she may go on to hurt themselves or someone else. This latter possibility raises concerns regarding public safety. How can society protect itself from being hurt by someone who is not getting the mental health treatment needed, while still respecting the basic human right of self-determination? As a case in point, how could society stop a potential "campus shooter" who refused his prescribed mental health treatment without sacrificing personal freedoms cherished by all?[6]

There is no simple solution to this dilemma. It helps for states to regularly review data from the enforcement of their commitment laws and ensure that these are functioning as intended—that there are few "false positives" and few "false negatives." It helps too for states to consider the concept of "outpatient commitment," which may require hospitalized, at-risk patients to continue their treatment in the home community as a prerequisite for early discharge.[7] Many of those who end up taking violent action would have been helped, and tragedy avoided, had they been placed in outpatient commitment. This would have assured that they continued receiving needed treatment in the home community, or, if necessary, were readmitted to inpatient care for further assessment and treatment. When this works well, it provides an alternative to the painful situation of a person with serious mental illness who is not at a place to accept help. Too often, families in such cases must watch helplessly as their loved one gets worse and worse until he or she finally meets the criteria for inpatient commitment. Outpatient commitment is designed to avoid just such pain.

But a deeper problem must be recognized in considering either inpatient or outpatient commitment—the quality of care. In those (hopefully) rare cases when the state determines that an individual must lose her freedom and be treated against her will, it is critical that the care received is appropriate, effective, and minimally restrictive. Otherwise, patients will understandably conclude that prescribed treatment is not in their own best interest. If hospitalization boils down to custodial care and overmedication to decrease symptoms, then patients are rightly going to jump at the first opportunity to be rid of treatment. Likewise, if after discharge the local community mental health center offers little more than a monthly "meds check" that continues the overuse of strong medications, discharged patients are likely to see this as more of a curse than a blessing. One problem with poor-quality mental health care is that it tends to overrely on psychotropic medications to manage symptoms and control behaviors.[8] It is not that these medications are not needed—they often are. But they should be used sparingly, and always in the context of responsive and flexible treatment (including psychotherapy if indicated) that takes into account the consumer's deepest needs and preferences. This is what Alison was rightly demanding. Had she not found alternative care, she would probably have dropped out of the mental health care system altogether, as many do.

So yes, there is a place for commitment laws, both inpatient and out-patient, but they cannot be successfully enforced unless the quality of mandated care is good. Otherwise, it is something like telling hungry and emaciated people that they must eat, then serving them spoiled food. It is not surprising that the starving people do not comply, even though we were right in saying that they need to eat. So here too, what is called for is the transformation of the entire broken mental health system of care. With intensive evidence-based inpatient services, even mandatory hos-pitalization can lead to positive outcomes. With effective and innovative, outcome-oriented community-based services leading to recovery, outpa-tient commitment becomes a viable option. Otherwise, all the best com-mitment laws in the nation will accomplish little.

One more factor to mention here is harder to articulate but very im-portant. That is the question of human dignity. Is it possible to implement inpatient or outpatient commitment using procedures that uphold the dignity of those committed? Of course. And on paper such procedures usually look quite reasonable. But in my experience, which has included having to hospitalize a number of my patients over the years, what looks good on paper can end up being pretty horrendous in reality. Just ask any-one who has been committed what the experience was like, and chances are you will hear, often with tears, how demeaning it was. Not only must we provide effective care for those in need of commitment, but we must also make sure that the manner in which such care is provided respects the dignity of the person being treated. What is the best way to determine whether current commitment procedures respect human dignity? Simply ask the patient for feedback upon discharge.

Consumers and Their Families

It would be so much easier if an effective and responsive mental health system of care were already in place. Then consumers and their families could simply choose the provider that best fit their needs, collaborate in the treatment and evaluation process, and move on to recovery. Instead, we must acknowledge that many persons with serious mental illness, whether in the public sector or the private sector, must fight an uphill battle throughout their treatment process. There may be limited cover-age, limited choice among providers, little involvement in the treatment process, and no opportunity to evaluate treatment effectiveness. Improvement may be slow, overmedication may be involved, and it may seem that no single provider is really in charge. What to do?

If one of my family members or I had a mental illness, I would start by appealing to a reputable advocacy organization such as the local chapter of NAMI or Mental Health America. I would want someone to explain to me in simple terms what my options were and where I would be likely to find the most effective care for my particular needs. Only then, armed with good information, would I feel prepared to engage the public- or private-sector provider system. I would then be sure to ask a lot of questions as to extent of coverage and provider availability and would spend some time "trying out" different providers until I found one that matched my needs. I would expect such a provider to include me in the decision-making process and to invite me to give regular feedback as to the effectiveness of his or her care. I would expect to recover my ability to function well in the home community before too long,[9] and if improvement was not forthcoming I would expect new efforts until the right treatment was found.

The trouble with this scenario is that it assumes that either consumers or their family members are willing and able to successfully advocate for effective care. Unfortunately, this is often not the case. The consumer may be wrestling with major depression or another disabling disorder and thus be unable to serve as self-advocate. And other family members may or may not be able to help out. In my experience, both with medical/surgical health care and with mental health care, there is a huge difference between those patients who have someone advocating for them and those who do not. Those with an advocate tend to receive markedly better care.

Consumers must therefore keep this in mind when in need of mental health services. Are you able to serve as a self-advocate? If not, see if a family member can help you out. If that's not possible, then turn to an advocacy organization to help not only with information but perhaps with representation as well. There is no shame in allowing others to advocate for you when you are temporarily unable to do so for yourself. However, it is equally important to remember that the time will come when you will be able to take over the advocacy role for yourself and that it is very important to do so. Ultimately, you must be in charge of your own treatment. It is your life—your future—that is at stake.

Many persons with serious mental illness, after recovery, are motivated to "give back" to others who may come to have the same needs they experienced. This is laudable, and one way to do so is to volunteer through an advocacy organization to help other consumers out as needed. The volunteers may find themselves helping another to navigate the same confusing mental health system they had to work through, an experience that can be as rewarding for the volunteer as it is helpful for another.

Mental Health Providers

As a licensed and practicing psychologist, I understand how frustrating it can be to have a patient question or even challenge my treatment decisions. It can slow the process of treatment and leave me feeling that my training and expertise are not being fully appreciated. What do all those diplomas on the wall mean—nothing? It's even worse when patients expect to improve at an unrealistic rate and blame me when that doesn't occur. Who are they to tell me that my treatment is not working as well as they had hoped? I do understand how frustrating this can be for providers, and I realize that sometimes it's the patient's illness speaking, but I have a simple response both for myself and for my fellow mental health providers—"get over it!" The sooner we make our peace with empowered, self-advocating consumers and advocates, the better off all will be. The days of autocratic health and mental health care are coming to an end, and on balance that is a good thing. The ultimate result of collaborative mental health care is improved clinical outcomes, which means that more consumers will recover more quickly and find their place in the home community more readily. That's worth providers having to tolerate a lot of potential frustration.

Collaboration must start at the first encounter. Whenever a new person is referred to my office for psychotherapy, I suggest that he or she may want to compare me with one or two other psychologists before making a final decision. The first meeting can thus be seen as a trial session for the patient to determine whether he or she would prefer to work with me as compared to others. Consumers tend to really appreciate this point and usually (but not always) come back to work with me. Those who do have made a choice that is beneficial for the treatment process. It means they are working with me not by default but by their own choice, which empowers them all the more to take an active role in their recovery. Additionally, I like to use standardized surveys that measure symptomatology, functionality, and overall satisfaction.[10] These can be as simple as the Beck Depression (or Anxiety) Inventory plus a question or two on level of functioning and satisfaction and can be given before, during, and at the end of treatment. This provides ongoing clinical data so that improvement can be tracked and so that it will be clear when treatment goals are met (e.g., no symptoms and full functioning at home, work, or school). As we have seen, both consumers and insurers appreciate the use of clinical outcome data to help guide the course of treatment.

There is as yet little financial imperative for mental health providers to invite consumer collaboration in the treatment process or to use standardized clinical outcome measures. Most clinicians work within fairly restricted referral systems and have not been required to provide standardized data for tracking patients' improvement. However, as we have seen, many voices are calling for a more market-driven system. A key component of a competitive environment is that consumers will have more choice among providers. Thus the day may soon come when a person struggling with serious mental illness will be able to choose between several options as to which treatment approach and which provider best meets his or her needs. Those providers who are open to consumer collaboration and who are willing to document effectiveness will flourish, while those who cling to the old autocratic and secretive approach to mental health care will not.

Therefore, now is the time for forward-looking mental health providers to begin offering what a transformed mental health care system will eventually require—collaborative, recovery-oriented, evidence-based, documented care.

Policy Makers

I have served as commissioner for Virginia's Department of Mental Health and as a National Advisory Council member for the nation's primary mental health services agency.[11] I have worked with numerous councils and commissions and committees charged with developing mental health policy. Those positions entailed dozens of meetings with other policy makers and, at times, with consumers and their advocates. It is probably true to say that meetings with no consumers or advocates present were shorter and easier. Decisions could be made simply on the basis of prior policies, current needs, and fiscal/political realities. Why complicate things further by having people present at the table who have a personal stake in the decisions reached? Is that not somehow inviting a conflict of interest? Doesn't it inevitably slow the process and frustrate all parties?

Yes and no. It is true that opening up a policy discussion to consumers and advocates can make it more difficult to reach a speedy conclusion. It is also true that some people are "professional consumers" and "professional advocates" who seem to live for such activities and make a career of showing up again and again in various meetings. Such persons are good-hearted but tend to be fairly strident and unreasonable in their demands. They are less likely to be able to accept "half a loaf," which is often what reality demands, and they sometimes have a hard time functioning as a team player. But there is another kind of consumer and advocate who is very valuable to the policy-making process—the everyday person who gets involved for a time simply out of concern for all those with mental disorders. These people should be sought out and prized, for they will contribute greatly to policy discussions. They will make sure the tough questions are addressed and will then work hard to find realistic ways to move forward. I know this from experience.

As mental health commissioner for the state of Virginia, I served in some respects as the primary mental health policy maker. It was my job to recommend to the governor and the legislature policies and funding proposals that would improve the quality of mental health care. When I began, I questioned whether it was really necessary to include mental health consumers and advocates in top policy discussions. Like many uninformed policy makers, I assumed that the difficulties entailed would outweigh the benefits. I have to admit that in the early days I did what I now regret seeing others doing. I included consumers and advocates at the table so I could say I had done it but without really paying much attention to what they had to say. However, over time I came to realize a simple truth—they knew things that my top advisors and I did not know about mental health care because they lived it day in and day out.

I'll never forget one meeting I held early in my tenure as commissioner that involved the department's top policy makers as well as consumers and advocates. The discussion concerned whether to begin offering the PACT services described above (before they had been implemented). One of the CMHC's executive directors stated in response to an advocate's questions that he knew PACT worked well and that such services could make a huge difference in the lives of persons who cycled in and out of state psychiatric hospitals. The advocate then asked the obvious: "So why in the world don't you offer those services?" To my amazement, the answer had to do with turf. In so many words, the executive director stated that he had his funds already dedicated to various favored programs (effective or not) and that nobody wanted to relinquish their funding for a new project. He also pointed out that hospitalization costs are not charged to the CMHC so there is little financial incentive to avoid using psychiatric inpatient care. The advocate was understandably furious and stormed out of the meeting, and I called for a break. During the break I tracked the advocate down and spoke with her about what had happened. Her passion for providing effective care, as well as her clear understanding of the usefulness of PACT services, changed me. I came away from that meeting convinced that we needed to really listen to what the consumers and advocates had to say. This was one reason I later supported the consumers' proposal to use $500,000 to test the PACT program. Some were pleasantly surprised that I took their suggestion so readily, but by then I was convinced that consumers and advocates were often more on target than the professional policy makers.

I encourage policy makers in the public and private mental health sectors to invite consumers and advocates to the table on a regular basis (if they are not already doing so). It is true that the process will be a little more complicated, and it is indeed possible to end up with someone who does not understand economic/political realities or who is not used to being a team player. But this is a risk well worth taking, simply because they know things you don't know. Listen to what they have to say even when it's outside the boundaries of what you're used to, even when it goes beyond the stated agenda. They see very clearly what we providers and policy makers see only in part—how tragically the mental health system fails to meet the critical needs of a person with serious mental illness and how lives and funds are needlessly wasted. So they are highly motivated to cut through the "BS" that often rationalizes status quo services and to consider new ways of doing things that professional policy makers would never dream of. Let them dream a little, take them seriously, and you just may find that your mental health policy proposals change significantly. You may find yourself eager to try something new, something that might actually make a huge difference in the lives of persons struggling with serious mental illness.

Integrated Care versus the "Carve-Out"

Another issue that must be considered when discussing the consumer's unique perspective in policy and treatment is America's "carved-out" mental health care system. This term refers to the fact that the mental health service system is largely separated from general medical/surgical health care services. Mental health professionals are often located away from general health care facilities, and psychiatric hospitals are often stand-alones (although some general hospitals have psychiatric wings). In most cases persons who need mental health services cannot go to their usual family doctor or community hospital. Instead, they must find a separate mental health professional or psychiatric hospital, both of which are outside the boundaries of typical health care needs. For many consumers, this is a confusing and difficult process and one that heightens the sense of stigma. Nobody asks any questions when you say you are on the way to the family doctor for a checkup. But if you say you are on your way to see a mental health professional, or receiving services at a psychiatric hospital, eyebrows are raised. Further, although many family doctors know a little about depression and can prescribe antidepressant medications, most are not trained to assess or treat mental illnesses.

The separate care systems not only keep people from seeking psychiatric care but can also keep people with serious mental illness from receiving needed medical care. Those who spend a lot of time with mental health providers tend to focus only on those needs. Important medical needs may go undetected or, even if known, unaddressed, since the medical care system can be yet another hurdle to cross. Thus there would be benefit both ways (for people needing psychiatric care and for psychiatric patients needing medical care) in an integrated health care system that included mental health care.

As it is, there are two parallel systems of care—medical/surgical and mental health/substance abuse. Accessing the former is usually fairly straightforward, whereas accessing the latter can be nightmarish. This problem has recently been addressed by the National Academies of Science in the form of a report from their highly regarded Institute of Medicine (2006, viii): "Mental and substance use problems and illnesses should not be viewed as separate from and unrelated to . . . general health care. The link between mental and substance-use problems and illnesses, and general . . . health care, is very strong. Improving our nation's general health . . . depends upon equally attending to . . . mental and substance-use conditions. [This] requires a fundamental change in how we as a society . . . think about and respond to these problems and illnesses."

The fundamental change referred to would ultimately mean reintegrating mental health care into the general health care system, something that is much easier said than done. But why is it this way? Why do we have a carved-out mental health care system in the first place? Like so many things, this began as good public policy designed to accomplish something important, yet brought with it unintended negative consequences.

When the Kennedy administration launched their CMHC initiative in the 1960s, it correctly recognized that the centers needed to be funded as stand-alone organizations. Why? Because otherwise funding intended for mental health services would easily migrate back into the general health care system. If community mental health services had been provided through general health clinics and hospitals in the 1960s, the effort would probably have failed because funds would inevitably end up being drawn into the organizations' primary mission—health care. Thus the mental health care system was "carved out" as a stand-alone so that it could survive in an environment that focused on and prized general health care. The CMHCs were required by law to be separate so that they could accomplish their work and, hopefully, flourish.

Unfortunately, it took decades for the centers' planned expansion to be adequately funded so that a center would be conveniently available for every community. Even now that is not fully the case, although the vast majority of counties nationwide do have a CMHC. Yet, thankfully, the basic purpose of a carved-out mental health system was accomplished, since a separate system of mental health services is now in place. Although the current system is broken and in need of transformation, at least it exists. The carve-out worked in that it allowed for something new to become well established.

Now, however, the limits of a stand-alone mental health system are showing. It is very hard to coordinate care for a person's mental health and substance use needs with care for his or her medical needs. Yet the two are often closely related, as stated above by the Institute of Medicine. Also, it is still hard to overcome the barriers to treatment resulting from stigma that are inherent in a carve-out. Consider the case of Ed.

"ED"

Ed was a young professional in the Los Angeles area who had survived a close call with pancreatic cancer three years ago. He worked for the aerospace industry and had excellent private health insurance from his employer, so when he went in for his annual physical he always got good service. This year, though, he brought a new issue to his family doctor—he seemed to be suffering from some sort of panic attacks. During the physical he told the doctor that he had had several times when his heart raced and he thought he was going to die, often had trouble sleeping, and felt generally on his guard at all times. Did this mean he had a mental disorder, or could it be something physiological? Could this perhaps be some sort of delayed reaction to the chemotherapy treatment he had endured? Ed had read something to that effect but did not know what to believe.

The doctor was attentive but had little expertise in mental illness. So he recommended that they add a few more blood tests to the usual array required for annual physicals, then talk again. A week later the nurse called Ed to tell him his blood work all looked good, so the doctor recommended that he see a mental health professional. Ed asked for a specific referral but was told that he needed to contact his insurer's vendor who handled mental health services, a different organization altogether. Ed already had mixed feelings about acknowledging that he was struggling with panic attacks, and it had taken a lot of effort just to bring it up to the doctor. Reluctantly he called the mental health vendor and scheduled an appointment. But when he drove up and found that the office was located on an out-parcel at a psychiatric hospital, he changed his mind. He turned around, went back home, and gave up on getting help. Instead, he decided to "tough it out," which meant that he endured his panic attacks for another six months until he finally found an outpatient clinic that specialized in anxiety disorders. Had he been treated earlier, he probably would have recovered within six weeks. Instead, he endured a heavy burden that was costly on him, his family, and his co-workers.

What would help? Suppose that Ed's doctor had a mental health professional who worked with him as part of the family practice. Ed could have been seen then and there, screened for anxiety disorders, and referred to an appropriate mental health professional (after the blood work was cleared). Perhaps the referral would have been to the office next door, dedicated to specialty services such as mental health and physical therapy. This would have been much more attractive to Ed, since it would have felt like a seamless provision of care for health and mental health needs. He would have received the treatment he needed, in settings where other health needs were addressed, and been the better off for it.

What the case of Ed shows is that the mental health carve-out, while necessary for the launching of a new mental health system, now gets in the way of effective care. There is a need to reintegrate medical/surgical and mental health care in a thousand ways so that, ultimately, they complement each other in a seamless provision of health services. This could be done without worry that such action would lead to the absorption of mental health services because the carve-out has worked: the need for mental health care has been acknowledged on a national level.

This matter must eventually be addressed for mental health system transformation to be fully completed. However, it is best seen as "step 2" in a two-step process. The first step is to transform mental health services through the fivefold recommendations made in this book. That will establish mental health care as effective and valuable for dramatically improving the quality of life of persons with serious mental illness. Once that has been accomplished, it will be easier for health care policy makers to turn their attention to the reintegration of mental health care with general medical services. Otherwise, it is something like asking a successful company (health care) to merge with a company about to file for bankruptcy (mental health care). Better to wait until there are two strong candidates for merger.

One way to help bring reintegration about is to give consumers and advocates a greater voice at the table of mental health policy development. Usually, this just means inviting a fair representation of those who will be affected by a given policy discussion to join in the dialogue early on. They will point out how troubling it is to navigate in a carved-out system of mental health care and how that gets in the way of recovery. They will remind policy makers that ultimately it is in everyone's best interest to build a truly integrated system of health care that includes both medical and mental health services as two sides of one coin. And they will be right.

Conclusion

This chapter, like the rest, is not meant as a stand-alone. It will not do much good for persons with serious mental illness to collaboratively engage the mental health service system if nothing changes. Why attempt to speak up in a system of care that is structured to ignore what you say? But if the time has really come to transform the mental health system of care, then theirs is the voice that is probably most needed as new treatments and payment structures are contemplated. Let the persons on behalf of whom these services are offered tell us when we have it right and when we do not. Let them have a say in selecting their provider, in making treatment decisions, and in assessing their own clinical outcomes. Let them be at the table where new mental health policies are hammered out. The mental health "experts" created the current mental health system, which is still trying to overcome the devastating consequences of poorly implemented deinstitutionalization. Perhaps if we pay more attention to consumers and advocates this time around, we will come closer to getting it right.

How would it look if we did get it right—if America's mental health care system were transformed into one that invited consumers and advocates to collaborate on policy and treatment, one that was outcome oriented and based on innovative community services, one that was not afraid to embrace evidence-based practices and accountability? Consider the following composite, hypothetical case intended to illustrate transformed, recovery-oriented mental health care.

"BILL"

Bill was a twenty-four-year-old who had been honorably discharged from the army two years previously after serving two tours in Iraq. Following discharge, he enrolled in a community college, where he had intended to work toward a business degree, but ended up dropping out of classes during his second semester. He had recently married (six months earlier) to Mary, whom he had met in college and whom he adored. He now worked as an auto mechanic at a dealership, the trade he learned while in the service, but was having difficulty keeping his job. His manager noticed that he sometimes came in late, smelling of alcohol, and warned him that such behavior could not continue. Bill's heavy drinking had led to many arguments at home, and Mary had often suggested that they seek help. But Bill was not inclined to do so and each time simply vowed to do better. Now, however, a new problem had arisen. Bill reported hearing voices telling him to do terrible things, to hurt people. This alarmed both of them, and when Mary insisted that they seek help, Bill reluctantly agreed.

Mary had no idea where help could come from and knew that Bill did not trust the local Veteran's Administration (VA) hospital where he went for regular medical services. He thought the doctors there were keeping an eye on him and hoping to sign him up again. So she called the VA, asked what to do, and found out there was a new patient advocate service designed to help with just such situations, created in response to consumer requests. They were invited to schedule a meeting if desired. Bill wanted Mary at his side, so the two of them met with the advocate and learned critical information that shaped the course of their treatment. It turned out the VA had changed its policy that had previously required mental health treatment only at VA hospitals. Instead, as a veteran Bill had coverage that would apply to the provider of his choice in the private sector, so long as that provider accepted VA reimbursement rates (which were set to match the local market). They even had a list of local mental health providers that Bill could work with. The advocate suggested that he try two or three before selecting the one that could best meet his needs and gave him a list of questions to ask to evaluate the quality and fit of care offered.

Bill ended up meeting with two psychologists and one psychiatrist, each time telling his story and then asking the questions that the advocate had suggested. Did the provider have experience and a good track record with the issues Bill was struggling with? Would medications be required, and if so how much? What therapy would be offered beyond medications? How long would treatment last? Would Bill be allowed to participate in treatment decisions? Would the provider regularly invite feedback on how well things are going? How could Bill and Mary learn more about the mental illness he was struggling with?

With Mary's input, Bill eventually selected a psychologist who had a lot of experience with veterans, who would refer out for medications as needed but rely primarily on psychotherapy, and who seemed open to full collaboration throughout the treatment process. After a comprehensive and in-depth assessment that took several visits, the psychologist told Bill he was dealing with two challenges: substance-induced psychotic disorder, and post-traumatic stress disorder (PTSD). In lay terms, Bill was traumatized from the horrors of warfare that he had experienced in Iraq and was constantly on edge, always anxious and on guard. As a result, he had learned to medicate his anxiety with alcohol but was now drinking so much that he was experiencing auditory hallucinations related to his PTSD. Therefore Bill needed to work on both areas—the drinking and the PTSD.

This was not an easy message for Bill to hear, and at first he balked, thinking that the psychologist was exaggerating. But after much discussion with the psychologist, sometimes (at Bill's request) involving Mary, he finally accepted the accuracy of the dual diagnosis. The psychologist lent Bill and Mary several books explaining his diagnoses and discussing treatment options. He could try to reduce his drinking on an outpatient basis using Alcoholics Anonymous (AA), psychotherapy, and possibly Antabuse.[12] Or he could enter a "detox" inpatient program first and follow up with AA and psychotherapy. The advantages and disadvantages of both options were discussed, and Bill eventually elected to use the detox program approach, since long-term results were often significantly better. However, this required some help with Bill's employer. Accordingly, with Bill's permission, the psychologist had a conversation with Bill's manager, who ended up offering paid leave for the duration of the week-long detox program. The psychologist had to document his diagnosis and the rate of improvement for Bill's insurer (the VA system), using measures sensitive to alcohol abuse and PTSD, on a monthly basis. He also had to assure them that he was using appropriate evidence-based treatment, in this case trauma-focused cognitive-behavioral therapy creatively coordinated with a community-based AA program.

Recovery was not easy for Bill, and there were several setbacks along the way. But with the support of his wife, with occasional help from the VA patient advocate, and with a provider who was both effective and collaborative, Bill ultimately overcame both his drinking and his PTSD. Eventually he was even able to return to college to earn the business degree he had always wanted.

Some may think the above scenario is Pollyanna-like, but it is not. It involves composites from several cases I have had over the years. The difference is that this hypothetical case puts together all the positive features of a transformed system of care as if it were so structured. It is actually not that difficult and not that expensive to offer innovative and effective care, compared to the status quo. But it does involve a radically different mind-set throughout the mental health service system—one that expects recovery from using evidence-based care, has insurer flexibility, and invites collaboration with consumers and their advocates.

What might have happened if Bill had not had the benefit of family support (Mary), advocacy (the VA patient advocate), a flexible insurer (the VA), and an effective provider (the collaborative psychologist)? He would likely sooner or later have lost control at home or work and been sent to a psychiatric hospital for evaluation. There, given his auditory hallucinations, it would have been easy to misdiagnose him with schizophrenia and start him on powerful antipsychotic medications. Once discharged, Bill probably would have stopped taking the medications because of their side effects and would have continued to go from bad to worse. He might even have acted on the voices telling him to hurt himself or others.

This hypothetical case simply illustrates what mental health consumers and advocates know already, that we must consider more than just how much it costs to provide effective mental health care. Yes, there is definitely a financial cost to be borne by the insurer, and accountability for the use of those funds is appropriate. But we must also consider how costly it is to *not* provide effective care for our friends, neighbors, and family members who struggle with serious mental illness. How many tragedies, personal or public, could be avoided? How much needless agony must individuals and families experience from the lack of effective care? How many lives of people who could have been (and wanted to be) productive members of their home community must be wasted because of a broken mental health care system? With consumers and advocates at the table for both policy-making and treatment decisions, such questions will not be overlooked. They will be front and center as policies are being drafted and as treatment is being provided. In this way, consumers and advocates provide a critical voice that must be heard—and taken seriously—if mental health reform is to succeed.

6

Transforming America's Mental Health System

The United States spends significantly more per person on health care that any other country but the evidence shows that care is often poor and inappropriate. Despite expenditures of over 1.9 trillion dollars—a cost that grows substantially every year—health care services remain fragmented and uncoordinated, and more than 46 million people are uninsured. Why can't America . . . produce higher quality care and better outcomes?

David Mechanic, *The Truth about Health Care* (2006, ix)

We envision a future when everyone with a mental illness will recover, a future when mental illnesses can be prevented or cured, a future when mental illnesses are detected early, and a future when everyone with a mental illness at any stage of life has access to effective treatments and supports—essentials for living, working, learning, and participating fully in the community.

The President's New Freedom Commission on Mental Health, *Achieving the Promise* (2003)

WE HAVE COME a long way since the opening statements of this book. We have defined serious mental illness and documented some of the failures of the current mental health system. We have pointed to the need for evidence-based practices and outcome-oriented care, as well as innovative community-based services. We have shown why monopolies don't work and what needs to be done to create a competitive mental health care system—one marked by high quality of care and a good selection of provider choices for consumers. We have noted the need for parity, for equal coverage for mental health care as compared with medical/surgical care, and for universal health care. And we have shown the need for a new and empowered collaborative role for consumers and advocates, one that provides the missing voice in policy and treatment decisions.

It has been insisted throughout this book that these changes cannot be applied piecemeal, as if from a cafeteria menu. They must be implemented together, as a whole, if mental health services are to be truly transformed. An incremental approach to reform has been tried for many years and is simply not getting very far (Grob and Goldman 2007; Olson 2006). Too many citizens who long to be part of the American dream are still consigned to a nightmare of poor access, ineffective care, minimal follow-up, and the vicious cycle of rotating in and out of treatment. To change this, a tipping point must be reached (Gladwell 2000), meaning that a convergence of efforts and changes suddenly adds up to something greater than just one more government or private-sector initiative that sounds good on paper but defaults back to the status quo in a few years. For real change to occur, all that is covered in this book (and perhaps more) must be implemented together. This will require remarkable leadership at many levels in both the public and private sectors. Men and women of vision and courage and skill who have compassion for persons with serious mental illness will have to step forward and do things that are risky. They will have to challenge the status quo in a major way, with no guarantee of success.

Overcoming Resistance

[Virginia's] Governor Jim Gilmore is trying again to close state mental health hospitals in Nottoway County, Danville, and Williamsburg. Once again, legislators from those areas say it won't happen. The incoming [Governor-elect] Warner administration hasn't decided what to do.

Michael Martz, "Mental Hospitals Back on the Block,"
Richmond Times Dispatch Reporter, January 11, 2002

The Commonwealth of Virginia has many historical firsts of which to boast, including the first psychiatric hospital opened in Colonial America (Eastern State, founded in Williamsburg in 1773). This is something to be proud of. It was built out of compassion for those with serious mental illness who had nowhere else to go. Since that time, Virginia has founded another fifteen state psychiatric facilities,[1] for a total of sixteen. Most of these facilities were built as large institutions, together originally able to house over fifteen thousand people with either mental illness or mental retardation. Today however, given the goals of deinstitutionalization and community-based care,[2] the total census stands at just under three thousand (distributed about half and half between persons with severe mental retardation and persons with serious mental illness). In other words, these facilities are running at about 20 percent of their original census capacity. Virginia now needs only a fraction of the sixteen psychiatric facilities she currently funds. Yet not one of the facilities has been closed despite efforts made by several governors and mental health commissioners, including myself. Why not? Because to do so would change the status quo, which is comfortable for those who benefit from it.

Each psychiatric facility is located in the district of a state senator and state delegate and provides a steady source of employment and political support (votes). For this reason, efforts to close a facility—even if the plan is to reinvest those same funds in needed mental health community services—are fought tooth and nail. During my tenure as commissioner, I proposed closing one of the sixteen facilities, retraining employees for community care (so that no jobs would be lost), and reinvesting facility funds into community services (so that no funding would be lost). Even so, I could not get the support of the legislature, since the members in whose district this facility lay opposed it. Other legislators tend to support their colleagues in such matters, knowing that one good deed deserves another. As the above quote shows, that same resistance continued after my tenure ended in 1997 and continues to this day. Yet if no facilities are ever closed in Virginia they will continue to drain well over half a billion dollars yearly from the mental health budget, severely limiting efforts to transform services into community-based care.

I mention this not to suggest that legislators in Virginia are more difficult than elsewhere—they are not. Rather, it is to illustrate the level of resistance to change that will meet any proposal for dramatic reform. Those who benefit from the status quo will predictably, and vigorously, resist any proposal for changes that could threaten current benefits. This applies not only to policy makers but to providers and insurers as well, and these challenges must be factored in as we consider what it would take to truly transform America's mental health care system.

There is no simple solution to overcoming resistance to change from the powers that be. In fact, many good people all over America are trying to do just that—to find some way to reform the mental health system despite the massive resistance such efforts call forth. As we have seen, several state mental health agencies are attempting to move ahead with the vision for a transformed, recovery-oriented mental health care system as portrayed in the final report of the President's New Freedom Commission on Mental Health (2003). In California, for example, about $1.5 billion of new funding annually has been dedicated to transforming the mental health system of care since 2004.[3] This is funding above and beyond the department's previous $3.5 billion annual budget—a unique fiscal resource for mental health reform. Yet the state still struggles to meet quality-of-care expectations, including the U.S. Department of Justice's civil rights criteria for state-run psychiatric hospitals.[4] The new funding is required by law to be used for new and much-needed community-based services, as opposed to funding more of the status quo. But there has been tremendous resistance to shifting funds from current favorite services and programs to innovative evidence-based practices.

It is understandably hard for mental health providers to be told that the way they do business must change; that they must offer evidence-based treatment, even if this means retraining; that they must document and report the actual clinical outcomes of their care; that they must collaborate with their clients in new ways. For many providers this seems far too burdensome for a profession that is already challenging, so change is deeply resented and firmly resisted.

Resistance can come from policy makers, providers, insurers (such as those who fight parity), and even in some cases the consumers themselves. Consumers may be misled (by those committed to the status quo) into believing that proposed changes will deprive them of what they want and need. They may have little opportunity to learn directly about the advantages reform would actually bring, especially if there is little or no educational campaign on the topic. Thus it is possible to have representatives from all mental health constituencies agreeing that system reform should be resisted, even though the proposed changes would have provided significant benefits for those receiving care.

What then can be done to move ahead with reforms that are desperately needed? Is America's mental health service system destined to remain mediocre and ineffective, with a few incremental reform efforts always chipping away at the edges but never really taking hold because of ongoing resistance? The answer is "yes"—unless a "perfect storm" of three factors occurs: visionary leadership, economic imperative, and public outcry. Only then will America have what it takes to implement the fivefold reforms proposed in this book. The good news is that storm clouds are already on the horizon.

Visionary Leadership

Leadership is a surprisingly difficult term to define, other than to say that it is a rare quality found in some men and women that makes it easy to follow them. Leadership guru Max DePree, who has written several very well-received books on the topics of leadership and management, says that "the first responsibility of a leader is to define reality" (DePree 2004, 11). What does this mean? If those in leadership positions care more about defending a comfortable status quo than accomplishing their mission, then the "reality" promoted is self-preservation above all else. But if a leader is vigorously attempting to find new ways to better accomplish the organization's mission, even at some risk to self, then those who follow will be inspired to do likewise. This can be called "visionary leadership," defined as seeing what could be and doing whatever it takes to bring it about. What America needs is visionary men and women who see clearly the failures of the current mental health system, who really understand and believe in what a recovery-oriented system would look like, and who will work tirelessly to get from the former to the latter. I believe there are a good number of leaders who do just that, who have what it takes in desire and talent to move the system ahead. Some elected officials (such as Senator Domenici, who sponsored the parity legislation referenced earlier), mental health commissioners, private sector CEOs, consumers and advocates, and providers are working hard on these very matters. But not enough! In my experience visionary leaders are vastly outnumbered by those who play it safe, who primarily want to manage their responsibilities in the ease of a comfortable status quo.

We must encourage visionary leadership among policy makers, providers, insurers (public and private), and consumer and advocacy groups. Given the needs and possibilities documented in this book, now is not a time for stability and predictability above all else. It is a time for innovative treatments to be tested, for evidence-based practices to be developed, for state monopolies to yield to competitive choices, for new funding mechanisms to be explored, for parity to be implemented throughout the mental health system, and for a truly collaborative approach to mental health care to be developed. It is a time for consumer recovery to become the stated goal for all those involved in the mental health system. This is the vision, and it is a good one. But visionary leaders must do more than articulate what could be. They must also be persistent and skillful in doing what it takes to get there. In my experience, effective visionary leaders are particularly competent at three things—collaboration, education, and strategic thinking.

Collaboration means reaching out to all those who have a stake in the matter at hand, whether or not they are one's natural allies. It is surprising how often those who oppose a given effort will respond well to an invitation to discuss the matter in an environment of mutual respect and civility. I found as mental health commissioner that it was not hard to cross the proverbial partisan aisle or to build friendships with those who initially opposed the very concept of mental health reform. Likewise, I found that stakeholders were glad to participate in roundtable discussions to determine together how to move the system forward with pilot projects. As a new commissioner, I must admit, I at first thought I could simply make unilateral decisions and move the system ahead quickly in that way. But thankfully I came to learn how foolish this is in a democratic society. The only way to move ahead with something as dramatic as mental health system transformation is to vigorously, and credibly, collaborate with all stakeholders.[5] It has to be a team effort. Visionary leaders are skilled at building teams through collaboration and finding ways to move ahead together.

Education is a high priority simply because misunderstandings and misinformation abound whenever changes are proposed. Visionary leaders know that great effort must be put into educating friend and foe alike as to what is being proposed and why and that ongoing dialogue is necessary throughout the process. I learned this from capable staff at the Virginia Department of Mental Health who convinced me that we needed to publish a regular newsletter detailing mental health reform efforts and inviting feedback. Once the newsletter was published and distributed, false rumors abated, and we could focus on holding open meetings with all stakeholders to discuss the actual proposals—as opposed to misconstrued fears. A visionary leader will make sure that all interested parties are given all the information they need to understand what is being proposed and to defuse the unfounded fears that will invariably arise whenever change is in the air.

Strategic thinking involves having the ability to come up with practical and creative ideas for overcoming obstacles. This is perhaps the most challenging part of visionary leadership, since missteps can be very costly. Everyone supports collaboration and education, but what about a risky strategic move designed to overcome resistance to change? If successful, the move looks brilliant. But if not, the leader who implemented it can look foolish and ineffective. Thus it is critical not only that strategic ideas be well formulated but that they work. For instance, when the mental health clinic in which I practiced in the early 1990s attempted to implement outcome measures (measuring the patients' clinical improvement every four sessions), the director initially found great resistance from most clinic clinicians. Nobody wanted the extra duty of collecting data or the fear that any documented poor outcomes might be used against them. So the clinic director proposed two strategic changes to make the plan more palatable. First, the survey data would be turned around quickly and put in the patient's chart so that the information could benefit the work of the clinician on a weekly basis, thus making it beneficial for case management. Second, the clinic director would promise that no punitive actions would result from data analysis. Any need for improvement would be handled with remediation such as training or mentoring. Thankfully the strategy was successful, clinicians cooperated, and the result was that outcome data tended to improve the clinic's overall quality of care. Had the strategy not worked, the director's ability to provide leadership in the clinic would have been diminished, at least for a time. Visionary leaders must think strategically, implement carefully, and be prepared to handle the associated risks.

Of course, other leadership factors could be mentioned, including the discovery that the most effective leaders tend not to be those with huge egos that must constantly be fed with praise and recognition but rather those with the humility to step back and let others flourish (Collins 2001; Lipman-Blumen 1996). Further, Max DePree (2004) has pointed out that followers respond best to leaders with clear values and high ethical standards applied consistently to themselves as well as their followers, even when it costs something (e.g., profit sharing with all employees). One could also mention the sheer courage that it takes for a leader to challenge the status quo in any setting. The visionary leader will have many laudable qualities that go beyond the scope of this book, but these three core competencies are essential, especially in a time of change. Unless the visionary leader is collaborative, educative, and strategic, he or she will not get far with reform.

One more aspect to visionary leadership must be mentioned, the need for it to go all the way to the top. Unless the highest levels of authority actively support mental health reform, it cannot succeed. In the public sector, this means that ultimately there is a need for presidential support for federal reforms and gubernatorial support for state reforms. In the private sector of providers and insurers, the CEO (and in most cases the board) must share the vision. With leadership that can be counted on from on high, those below can afford to take the risks necessary to bring about real change. Without it, it is just a matter of time until lower-level leaders are told to back off rather than trouble the numbing but comfortable stasis of the status quo.

Economic Necessity

My father was an economist, and he used to say that economics is the "dismal science" because it demonstrates that all major policy decisions are actually driven by financial considerations, regardless of what policy makers may say. Hopefully that is an overstatement, but it points to an important truth. Unless maintaining the status quo becomes more costly than changing it, nothing will change. The bad news is that our society is indeed in large measure economically driven. The good news is that America is at a point where the economic imperative for mental health reform is already visible.

America's health care system is in crisis. If you do not believe it, just try typing "health care crisis" on an Internet search engine (such as Google), and note the number of hits. Having backed off from managed care constraints (because of customer complaints), insurers are finding that medical costs are once again going through the roof. Many companies are shrinking employee health plans to control costs or even forgoing coverage altogether. Patient out-of-pocket expenses such as deductibles and co-payments are rising yearly. Insurance premiums doubled from 2000 to 2008. More and more people lack health insurance, with estimates as high as forty-six million (Mechanic 2006). Universal health care coverage is being promised by an increasing number of politicians, including President Obama, but there is no agreement on how to bring it about or how to pay for it.

Mental health care, as a subset of general health care, is no better off. Well over $69 billion is spent every year on mental health services (Office of the Surgeon General 1999), yet with too little to show in results. A quarter of all social security payments are for persons with mental illness (Rosenberg 2008). America spends 16 percent of its GDP on health care (in contrast, no other country spends more than 10 percent), with an increasing portion related to mental illness. Medicaid and Medicare, the government insurers that cover much of the costs of mental health care in the public sector, cannot sustain current growth rates in expenditures. Taxes will have to be raised or programs cut if the status quo continues. To add insult to injury, fewer than half of current mental health care services are supported by good evidence (Rosenberg 2008). Thus it is not at all clear that effective treatments are always purchased with the funds provided.

On the other side of this looming health care crisis, America endures increasingly powerful lobbying on behalf of those with vested interests who by nature resist reforms. The pharmaceutical, hospital, and doctors' associations spend tens of millions of dollars each year lobbying state and federal legislators to ensure that no legislation is passed that would threaten their own financial interests.

And just to complicate matters further, America is now enduring an economic downturn triggered by subprime mortgages that greatly reduces the total revenue available for social needs of any sort. This simply raises the stakes for all those with vested economic interests. Everyone must fight even harder to hold onto their portion of the economic pie.

As a result, there is a growing tension between those who argue for more of the same (plus increased funding) and those who are calling for radical reforms. Exactly how long this standoff will continue is unpredictable, but it cannot go on indefinitely. Given the unsustainable rise in health care costs, the current economic crisis, the push toward universal coverage, and the growing recognition that even expensive treatments are too often not effective, a tipping point will soon be reached. At that point financial pressures will force policy makers to consider implementing real change whether or not they are so inclined. How can universal coverage, complete with parity for mental health, possibly be implemented without breaking the bank and adding to the nation's economic woes? It can only be done if the quality and effectiveness of mental health care are radically transformed in the manner addressed in this book. It can only be done if the services paid for are outcome oriented, evidence based, offered in a competitive environment, focused on recovery, and accountable. If can only be done if consumers get what they (or their insurers) are paying for.

When that happens, when changes in payment structures and expectations for providers are implemented, mental health providers will be faced with a stark choice. Either they will have to make their peace with outcome-oriented, recovery-focused, collaborative community care, or they will not be able to survive financially. Given human nature to hold onto whatever is comfortable as long as possible, and thus to resist changing the status quo, this financial imperative is a necessary factor for mental health system transformation. Certainly many enlightened mental health providers are ready and willing to embrace the call for recovery-oriented care, even if that requires some retraining and changes in clinical practice. But many more are not, and for them economic necessity is indeed a necessary factor for change to occur.

My father may have a point about economics invariably driving change, but in this case it could work to everyone's advantage. The realities of today's economic and health care crises are likely to become primary drivers for much-needed and long-overdue mental health reform.

Public Outcry

The third component of the perfect storm for mental health transformation has to do with the American public—their outcry over the sad state of affairs for citizens with serious mental illness. Only sustained public outcry can overcome a politician's tendency to play it safe and follow the suggestions of various powerful lobbying groups. Only public outcry can bring the nation to a tipping point such that real and lasting changes in mental health care can be implemented across the board—at federal and state levels, in public and private sectors, among insurers and providers alike.

A good example of this dynamic is the antismoking movement of the 1970s and 1980s, which succeeded in absolutely transforming the nation's perception of and tolerance for smoking. Whereas previously tobacco industry lobbyists had successfully resisted calls for changes in advertising and considerations of liability, all of that has now been turned around 180 degrees. Who would have thought in the early 1970s that most of corporate and retail America would transform itself into smoke-free environments? Who would have thought that ads glorifying smoking for all would become a thing of the past? Our society now assumes that smoking is harmful and is not hesitant to proclaim that fact in everything from elementary textbooks to discussions on the liability of "secondary" smoke (being near others who smoke). Without sustained public outcry over the tobacco industry's contribution to health problems, through the media as well as through judicial decisions from individual and class-action suits, these changes would not have occurred.

Of course, the call for mental health reform does not naturally appeal to as wide an audience as the call for smoking cessation. But that could change. There are several potentially potent public concerns regarding mental health issues that currently seem unrelated. But if the public came to see that the underlying issue was the same in all cases (ineffective or unavailable treatment), and if the media picked up on it in a sustained manner, a tipping point could be reached. This applies to concerns for the "homeless mentally ill," public safety concerns regarding untreated mental illness (including lack of treatment for those in jail), concern for Iraq veterans suffering from PTSD and other mental health problems, and concern for the plight of persons with serious mental illness caught in the vicious cycle of ineffective treatment and predictable relapse.

Estimates of homelessness in America vary, in part by how the term is defined, to up to seven hundred thousand people on any given night and over 3.5 million throughout the course of a year (National Alliance to End Homelessness 2000). In light of the subprime mortgage crisis and the skyrocketing rate of home foreclosures, those numbers are likely to be much higher today. Whatever the number may be, there is a growing public awareness that it is far too high and that a significant proportion consists of those who struggle with serious mental illness. In fact, one estimate is that up to two-thirds of homeless adults struggle with chronic alcoholism, drug abuse, mental illness, or some combination (Rosenberg 2008). Major newspapers have run compelling stories detailing the problem and following the grim daily life of people on the street. In most major cities much of the population is all too aware of the growing number of homeless persons, many of whom are mentally ill, and the need to do something about it.

Public safety concerns are front and center for the American public whenever a campus or mall shooter turns out to be a person with serious mental illness who is no longer in treatment. Concerns are also raised over mentally ill adults and adolescents who are incarcerated without access to treatment. The public is increasingly aware that persons with serious mental illness need effective treatment not only for their own sake but also for the sake of others and that the lack of such treatment puts many at risk.

It is a sad hallmark of war that veterans return from the front lines not only with physical wounds but also with psychological wounds. The unseen wounds are just as real and demand just as much attention. The nation was justifiably outraged and demanded change when it was discovered that Iraq veterans were receiving poor care at Walter Reed Hospital in Washington, D.C. There is a growing awareness that, despite improvements since, too many veterans are not being effectively treated for PTSD and other mental disorders triggered by their tour of duty. Most Americans feel it is simply not acceptable to fail to provide effective mental health treatment for those who have fought to maintain our freedoms.

Although stigma has long kept mental illness hidden as a topic for policy debate, this is beginning to change due to antistigma and educational campaigns over the past thirty years. More and more people recognize that mental illness could strike anyone and that they have friends and family members who struggle with depression, anxiety disorders, or other mental disorders. Consequently, there is a growing sense of sympathy for the many persons with serious mental illness who end up caught in a vicious cycle of ineffective treatment and inevitable relapse. Poor care is usually due either to low-quality services that are not evidence based or unavailability of treatment altogether. Increasing numbers of Americans feel that it is time to fix the mental health care system for the sake of those caught in it, even if that means spending more.

Each of these concerns currently falls short of hitting a tipping point regarding public opinion. However, it is probably just a matter of time until a tragic event changes that—until a catalyzing story focuses the nation's attention on the need for effective mental health care. Were that to occur, and were the underlying link among all of these concerns (i.e., ineffective or unavailable treatment) to become well recognized, then the necessary tipping point could be reached. At that point, sustained public outcry over the need to fix the mental health system once and for all could have the same effect that concerns over smoking had in the 1970s. It could motivate policy makers to support radical and even sweeping reforms that otherwise would seem too politically risky. It is a sad commentary that it takes a tragedy to galvanize the nation into action, yet too often that seems to be the case.

It is important to note that the "fourth estate"—the media—invariably plays a critical role regarding public outcry. Investigative reporting and sustained topical interest are invaluable assets without which the public is unlikely to coalesce around a cause. It is also true that strategic legal actions, including class-action suits, can be instrumental in the process of change, as they were in the case of the tobacco industry.

The Perfect Storm

Resistance to change is a natural human phenomenon, but it needn't be the final word when it comes to transforming the mental health system of care. With the perfect storm of visionary leadership, economic necessity, and public outcry, dramatic and far-reaching changes become possible. In each of these areas there are promising signs. An increasing number of federal and state mental health officials, as well as mental health consumers and providers, are calling for reform. The health care crisis and the move toward universal coverage are already providing an economic and political rationale for dramatic changes in health care and mental health care alike. President Obama and many congressional leaders have promised the American people that these critical matters will be addressed. And public awareness of the ethical and practical imperatives for providing high-quality care for persons with serious mental illness is growing by the day. It is impossible to predict exactly when the tipping point will be reached, but it is just a matter of time. And when that time comes Americans will roll up their sleeves and work together to transform the current failed mental health care system into one that will do the job—one that will provide what it takes for persons with serious mental illness to recover their ability to have a real home, a fulfilling job, and deep relationships.

Summary and Recommendations

The previous chapters have covered a lot of ground, so it is helpful to recap highlights and summarize recommendations. It is hoped that doing so will make this book useful not only for encouraging the goal of mental health transformation but also for developing a specific plan of action that fits the reader's needs.

Definitions and Vision for Transformation

We must define mental illness and serious mental illness in terms that make sense both clinically and from a public policy perspective.

Mental illness is a biopsychosocial brain disorder characterized by dysfunctional thoughts, feelings, and/or behaviors that meet diagnostic criteria listed in the *Diagnostic and Statistic Manual of Mental Disorders (DSM-IV)*.

Serious mental illness is based on two factors, diagnosis and level of functioning, and includes six categories of mental disorders:

1. Psychotic disorders (e.g., schizophrenia)
2. Mood disorders (e.g., bipolar disorder, major depression)
3. Anxiety disorders (e.g., panic disorder)
4. Childhood disorders (e.g., attention deficit/hyperactivity disorder)
5. Eating disorders (e.g., anorexia)
6. Substance-related disorders (e.g., alcohol dependence)

A person experiencing a serious mental illness will not only meet the criteria for a disorder in one of the six categories listed but also have significant difficulty functioning at home, work, or school.

Substance use disorders require treatment. We must treat not only mental illness but also substance use disorders, since the two are often related. Regardless of how responsible those struggling with substance use may or may not have been at one point, it is clear that once addicted they need help. It is also obvious that to not provide help is to leave such a person in a state that is dangerous for self and costly for society. So from both an ethical and a pragmatic point of view it makes good sense to offer effective substance use treatment along with other mental health services.

Less serious mental health needs must also be addressed, something that is often better accomplished by corporations, schools, religious institutions, and nonprofits:

- Corporations often offer their workers employee assistance programs (EAPs) that provide resources for managing stress, anxiety, anger, and grief.
- Schools can provide timely evaluation and appropriate support for children whose conduct is problematic, even while maintaining the importance of personal responsibility and parental involvement.
- Churches, synagogues, and mosques can play a critical role in ministering to members who are struggling with mental health needs. Many churches, for example, offer support groups and personal/pastoral counseling for those in need, as well as twelve-step programs.
- Nonprofits such as the Boy Scouts and Girl Scouts, sports clubs, and other community-based organizations often play an important supportive role in the lives of those who are faced with mental health needs.

A fivefold vision for mental health transformation is required if change is to be comprehensive and lasting. Otherwise, improvement will be piecemeal and temporary. A transformed mental health care system must be results oriented, innovative, consumer focused, well funded, and committed to change.

1. *Results oriented:* Using results-oriented outcome measures and "evidence-based practice" so as to improve quality of care and system accountability.
2. *Innovative:* Opening the monopolistic state mental health system to competition and innovation so as to improve effectiveness and increase treatment choices.
3. *Adequately funded:* Implementing "parity" so that mental health treatment coverage matches medical/surgical coverage, per the 2008 parity law.
4. *Consumer focused:* Empowering persons with serious mental illness—giving them and their families a real voice in policy development and service evaluation.
5. *Committed to change:* Overcoming resistance to change from forces wedded to the status quo.

How to Measure Progress

Less than half of all mental health care is supported by good evidence. The way forward is to measure actual clinical outcomes in the lives of those receiving mental health treatment. Scientifically sound and easy-to-use clinical outcome measures are readily available for just about any mental health service setting. An increasing number of policy makers and public/private insurers are expecting that treatments or services offered for a person with mental illness will first be subjected to scientific outcome-oriented testing and found to be effective. All mental health treatments will eventually be evidence based, and the expected outcome will be recovery.[6]

Although some policy makers, providers, consumers, and insurers resist embracing clinical outcome measures, their concerns (though understandable) can be addressed. It is well worth addressing them, since the potential for outcome-oriented improvement in quality of care, and in consumer recovery, will greatly benefit all parties. Following are recommendations for each stakeholder group.

Policy makers must recognize that now is the time to enact legislation to transform the mental health system, even if doing so carries some political risk. Specifically, policy makers should implement legislation or regulations to

- Require the regular use of standardized, objective, and uniformly applied clinical outcome measures (such as NOMs) and link the availability of outcome data to continued funding.
- Require the resultant outcome data (aggregated and without any identifying information) to be made available.
- Stipulate that outcome data are to be used in a remedial manner.
- Adequately fund the cost of implementing clinical outcome measures.
- Stipulate which agency or office will regularly review and analyze the resultant clinical outcome data.

Providers must embrace the call for evidence-based practice and become competent with the use of ongoing, standardized outcome data as a means for ensuring quality of care. Specifically, providers should

- Move ahead now with using clinical outcome measures, rather than waiting until insurers require such data as a matter of course.
- Market the fact that their practice uses scientifically validated clinical outcome measures as an indication that their services are a "cut above."
- Include the consumer's outcome data in requests for authorization for additional care (assuming full confidentiality is completely assured).

Consumers must see that focusing on their own clinical progress ensures a quality of care that is sadly lacking today and that this is one way to meaningfully collaborate in the treatment process. Specifically, consumers should:

- Regularly review their clinical status with their service provider and expect improvement.
- Ask for standardized clinical outcome information when selecting a specific program or treatment service to make sure that it's effective.

- Get involved with advocacy organizations such as NAMI or Mental Health America for helpful information and support.

Insurers must recognize the potential for improving quality of care, as well as the bottom line, by funding only evidence-based, effective treatments. They must also recognize that it is well worth paying more for high-quality services, including covering the additional costs entailed in measuring clinical outcomes. Specifically, insurers should

- Develop pilot projects to test the actual cost/benefit ratio of implementing outcome-oriented care.
- Move to full deployment by requiring all mental health providers to use the pilot-tested instruments and procedures.
- Seek support (tax incentives, etc.) from relevant state government and/or regulatory agencies for innovative mental health care.
- Market being on the "cutting edge" of high-quality care by moving into outcome-oriented services.

The national vision for outcome-oriented mental health system reform is a good one—to create effective home- and community-based services in place of custodial hospital care and to expect recovery as the result of effective care. But if America is really going to transform a moribund system of mental health services, it must have the courage to put a critical missing component in place—standardized, objective clinical outcome measures uniformly applied. Without the ongoing flow of data these measures provide, it is impossible to know to what extent community-based services are truly operational and working as intended. Once outcome data are made available, policy makers, providers, consumers, and insurers alike will be able to tell what is working, for whom, and in what setting.

Creating a Competitive Market

There is no inconsistency between vigorous competition and the delivery of high-quality health care. In fact, when vigorous competition prevails consumer welfare is maximized. Yet a state mental health agency is by definition a monopolistic enterprise. The inherent monopoly of state mental health agencies must be broken, much as the railroad and oil monopolies of the late 1800s had to be broken, if transformation is to proceed. Breaking the monopoly of state agencies would significantly improve the lives of those receiving care. Following are two strategies and five factors that together will create a truly competitive mental health system.

First strategy—link comparative data and funding. Use political "market forces" by comparing and contrasting the performance of mental health agencies across all states. Each state should be required to use the same standardized clinical outcome measures, apply them regularly to all persons receiving mental health care, and publicly report the resultant data (aggregated so as to avoid any identifying information). This will motivate states to do their best lest they be seen in a poor light in contrast with their "competitor" states.

SAMHSA is the primary services-oriented federal mental health agency. It funds a small but significant portion of mental health care in each state and should require normative outcome data in return for those federal funds. SAMHSA must stipulate that outcome data will be used only to guide technical assistance and other remedial resources and not for punitive purposes.

Second strategy—develop multiple providers. State agencies must contract with multiple providers who will be allowed to compete for a specific market of mental health consumers seeking the same category of care. If several state-funded providers offer the same category of mental health care, then market forces come into play and the providers will be keenly interested in competing well to attract those consumers who need their services.

State legislators must pass bills requiring that their mental health agency contract with at least two providers for each category of service offered, in such a way as to ensure that genuine competitive market forces are in play. Once such an environment is in place and providers are competing for the privilege of providing care, service quality will improve and costs will be kept reasonable through market forces.

A competitive mental health market requires five factors that, added to the two strategies listed above, will create a healthy market for effective care. If several of these conditions are not met, as is the case in most if not all states, then competitive market benefits are lost altogether.

1. *Well-informed consumers.* Mental health consumers must be able to learn about the quality and cost of services offered by various providers. Effort needs to be made to educate potential mental health consumers as to what their options are and what tends to be most effective for a given mental illness. In the private sector, insurance

companies should offer help in the form of a benefits counselor who works with an individual or their family needing mental health care until they have found the right treatment. In the public sector, there are mental health advocates who serve a similar role. In both cases, the result is a better informed consumer who is therefore more likely to find effective care—which benefits all parties. State legislatures should require such services in both the public and private sectors, knowing that the result will be improved quality of care and less "down time" for those struggling with serious mental illness.

2. *Price-sensitive consumers.* There must be incentive to search for mental health providers who offer the best service for the time and resources spent. In both the private and public sectors, the use of vouchers would be helpful. States should introduce a voucher system giving public-fund-eligible patients a certain amount to draw on per year for treating their mental illness. The amount must vary on the basis of diagnosis, severity, and average cost of local mental health services. There must be a review and appeals system in place to handle unique cases. Vouchers allow the mental health consumer to become more price conscious, and as a result the market will respond by promoting an array of competitive providers. State legislatures should call for pilot projects to test the helpfulness of vouchers for mental health care in both private-sector and public-sector settings.

3. *Well-informed sellers.* Mental health providers must know a lot about their customers—their needs and preferences. This means providers must keep up with the field and take training in new treatment approaches when relevant, as well as listen carefully to the patient's perspective so as to provide whatever best matches the patient's unique needs and preferences. Currently it is all too easy to hold onto mental health patients as long as possible, even if treatment does not seem to be helping as much as expected. The market must reward those providers who work hard to make sure that all patients get the most effective and efficient care possible, even if that means referring out. This requires the provider to supply information on the type and duration of services provided, the actual clinical outcomes in the lives of the patients, the extent to which the provider refers to other specialists, and the effort made to keep well trained in evidence-based practices (e.g., continuing education). Such information could be made available (e.g., on the Web) to potential

patients, who could then make informed decisions as to who would likely best meet their needs. State legislatures should phase in such requirements over several years for those seeking licensure as a mental health professional. During the phase-in time, states should offer technical assistance and training for providers.

4. *Easy market entry and exit.* It must be fairly easy for mental health providers to enter profitable markets and exit unprofitable ones (yet in a way so as not to disrupt care). Both public- and private-sector mental health organizations must streamline and redesign contracting processes so as to encourage innovation and support creative new ideas for helping persons with serious mental illness recover their ability to live successfully in their home community. Innovative new potential contractors must be welcomed as friends and helped through the submission process, rather than kept at arm's length.

5. *Avoidance of monopoly.* There must be an option for competitive mental health providers to enter the market and offer similar services at lower cost and/or higher rate of effectiveness. For this to be ensured, it is critical that antitrust laws be in place, that they be enforced, but that enforcement be managed with wisdom. The goal is not just to enforce the laws per se but to ensure that a competitive mental health care market thrives, producing high-quality services that are as effective as they are efficient.

In conclusion, both the private and public sectors need leadership that is committed to open and fair competition and willing to push that agenda. The CEO of an insurance company or the commissioner of a state department of mental health must be convinced that competitive provider market forces will improve quality of care and that the battle to overcome monopolistic tendencies is worth the fight. For the sake of all Americans with serious mental illness, let us determine to do away with the monopolistic stranglehold over mental health care with the same zeal with which railroad monopolies were overcome.

How to Ensure Adequate Coverage for Mental Health Care

The transformation of mental health services will not get far if those with serious mental illness lack the coverage necessary to receive needed care. Individuals and families that already struggle with the effects of serious mental illness should not have to struggle financially as well. Thankfully, the 2008 mental health parity law, if implemented effectively, will go a long way toward reducing this burden. However, "The devil is in the details," and it is critical that federal and state policy makers see this through carefully and with accountability. The new funds must be used to advance mental health reform, not just to grow the status quo. Only then will we achieve the high quality of care and positive clinical outcomes that patients and their families deserve and demand.

Clinical necessity should replace medical necessity for mental health services. Clinical necessity can be defined as a set of criteria to determine when a patient with serious mental illness is in need of services. The following definition of clinical necessity is offered, on two levels. The words in parentheses shift the definition from "all mental illness" to "serious mental illness." To qualify for payment per clinical necessity, mental health services must be

- For the treatment of (serious) mental illness and substance use disorders, or symptoms of these disorders, and the remediation of (significant) impairments in day-to-day functioning related to them, or
- For the purpose of preventing the need for a more intensive level of mental health and substance abuse care, or
- For the purpose of preventing relapse of persons with (serious) mental illness and substance use disorders, and
- Consistent with evidence-based, generally accepted clinical practice for mental and substance use disorders, and
- Efficient, in the sense of preferring a less expensive but equally effective treatment where possible, and
- Not for the patient's or provider's convenience

The primary difference between medical necessity and clinical necessity is that the first three bullets are "or" phrases. This means treatment can be deemed clinically necessary to treat symptoms, *or* to prevent more serious mental illness, *or* to prevent relapse.

Preventive care is critical for a transformed mental health care system. With clinical necessity a longer-term view is required, one that includes prevention of relapse and worse problems down the road. Strict medical necessity, applied to mental health care, often has unanticipated negative cost consequences. It is necessary to assess for and address long-term needs so that long-term costs may be minimized.

Universal health care, and the uninsured, must also be addressed for mental health reform to succeed. Two comments can be made from the perspective of a transformed mental health care system. First, unless the problem of the uninsured is solved, mental health reform can succeed only in part. Universal coverage would mean that anyone with serious mental illness could receive the treatment they need and avoid ending up at emergency rooms, on the street, or in prison. Without it, a large number of those in need will not be treated regardless of parity or other reforms and will continue to live out the tragedy of serious mental illness unaddressed. Second, if the health care and mental health care systems are reformed, then some streams of funding will become available to help cover the costs of universal health care. For instance, many hospitals currently receive significant yearly funding called "disproportionate share" that is intended to reimburse the cost of care for uninsured patients. Such funds could of course be reduced if there were few uninsured patients.

It is time for America to address the problem of so many citizens living without the benefits of health insurance. It may not be a basic human right, but reasonable coverage for all makes sense on many levels, both ethically and economically. More to the point of this book, it provides a scenario within which mental health transformation can succeed for all citizens rather than a select portion.

How to Build a Collaborative Mental Health System

The mental health advocacy movement is growing throughout the world and is starting to bring about major changes in the way persons with mental illness are regarded. Consumers are beginning to articulate their own vision for the services they want and need and to make increasingly informed decisions about their own treatment. Yet we have a long way to go. Too many persons with mental illness still feel disenfranchised and disempowered by the way they are treated when seeking care. They and their families are shuffled from one provider to another and told what to do, without being able to participate in the decision-making process for their own care. Further, they are typically left out of policy and program deliberations. They are often not at the table when new programs are being contemplated, when policies are being drafted, or when treatments are being evaluated for effectiveness. Instead, consumers and family members alike tend to be brushed off and told that the experts must decide these matters.

Recent research, however, has pointed out an embarrassing fact—that many decisions made by well-meaning but hard-pressed health professionals are in fact erroneous. Psychologists, psychiatrists, social workers, and others are trying to provide what will best fit the patient's needs. But nobody is perfect. Therefore it is actually in everyone's best interest for the mental health professional to engage the patient in meaningful dialogue about treatment options before prescribing care. It also makes good sense to invite regular feedback from patients as to how well they're doing and how satisfied (or not) they are with treatment.

The top priority should be to empower and equip patients and their families to take a more proactive role in the recovery process. This means inviting persons with serious mental illness and their families to collaborate in everything from policy making to treatment decisions to service evaluation.

Collaborative Care for Consumers

If you or one of your family members had a mental illness, you should start by appealing to a reputable advocacy organization such as the local chapter of NAMI or Mental Health America. You would want them to explain in simple terms what your options are and where you would be likely to find the most effective care for your particular needs. Only then, armed with good information, will you be ready to engage the (public- or private-sector) provider system. You should then be sure to ask a lot of questions as to extent of coverage and provider availability and to spend some time "trying out" different providers until you find one that matches your needs. You should expect such a provider to include you in the decision-making process and to invite you to give regular feedback as to the effectiveness of his or her care. You should expect to recover your ability to function well in the home community before too long, and if improvement is not forthcoming you should expect new efforts until the right treatment is found.

Consumers must keep this in mind when in need of mental health services. Are you able to serve as a self-advocate? If not, see if a family member can help you out. If that's not possible, then turn to an advocacy organization for help not only with information but perhaps with representation as well. There is no shame in allowing others to advocate for you when you are temporarily unable to do so for yourself. However, it is equally important to remember that the time will come when you will be able to take over the advocacy role for yourself, and it is very important to do so. Ultimately, you must be in charge of your own treatment. It is your life—your future—that is at stake.

Collaborative Care for Providers

Regarding the increasing role for consumers in mental health care treatment and policy, I have a simple response both for myself and for my fellow mental health providers—"get over it!" The sooner we make our peace with empowered, self-advocating consumers and advocates, the better off all will be.

Collaboration must start at the first encounter. You should suggest that a new patient may want to compare you with one or two other providers before making a final decision. The first meeting can thus be seen as a trial session for the patient to determine whether he or she would prefer to work with you as compared to others. Consumers tend to really appreciate this point, and many if not most will choose to work with you. Those who do have made a choice that is beneficial for the treatment process. It means they are working with you not by default but by their own informed decision, which empowers them all the more to take an active role in their recovery. Additionally, you should use standardized surveys that measure symptomatology, functionality, and overall satisfaction. These can be as simple as the Beck Depression (or Anxiety) Inventory plus a question or two on the topics of functioning and satisfaction and can be given before, during and at the end of treatment. This provides ongoing real-time clinical data so that improvement can be tracked and so it will be clear when treatment goals are met (e.g., no symptoms and full functioning at home, work, school, etc.). Both patients and insurers appreciate the use of clinical outcome data to help guide the course of treatment.

Collaborative Care for Policy Makers

I encourage policy makers in both the public and private mental health sectors to consider inviting consumers and advocates to the table on a regular basis. Let them dream a little, take them seriously, learn from them, and you just may find that your mental health policy proposals change significantly. You may find yourself eager to try something new, something innovative, something that might make a huge difference in the lives of persons struggling with serious mental illness.

Of course, there are risks involved. It's not always easy to have single-issue advocates around the table who may or may not agree with you. And innovative ideas may or may not be successful. But given the problems inherent in the status quo mental health system, and the growing impetus for radical reforms, these risks are well worth taking and will pay off in the long run.

Let Them Speak

The time has come to transform the mental health system of care, and the voice of consumers and advocates must be heard if new treatments and payment structures are contemplated. Let the persons on behalf of whom these services are offered tell us when we have it right and when we don't. Let them have a say in selecting their provider, in treatment decisions, and in assessing their own clinical outcomes. Let them be at the table where new mental health policies are hammered out. The mental health "experts" created the previous mental health system, which is still trying to overcome the devastating consequences of deinstitutionalization implemented without effective community-based care. Perhaps if we pay more attention to consumers and advocates this time around, we will come closer to getting it right.

It's actually not that difficult and not that expensive to offer innovative and effective care, compared to the status quo. But it does involve a radically different mind-set throughout the mental health service system— one that expects recovery through using evidence-based care, has financial flexibility, and invites collaboration with consumers and their advocates. Consumers and advocates provide a critical voice that must be heard and taken seriously if mental health reform is to succeed.

Conclusion

We stand at the edge of history regarding the future for persons with serious mental illness. Custodial care and ineffective treatments that lead to wasted lives could become a thing of the past. The winds of change are blowing, and the bright light of new ideas is sometimes illuminating the way, sometimes blinding us. Some are calling for immediate radical transformation of the mental health system; others work hard to resist reform at all costs. Some acknowledge that the status quo is broken but are afraid to move ahead unless an easy path forward can be guaranteed. The way forward will not be easy, and transforming a broken system of care into one that works will take time. However, we can be confident that if we start moving in the right direction, if we are willing to do what it takes, and if we persist, then the goal of a recovery-oriented mental health care system will eventually be attained. This book lays out what that direction looks like, through the fivefold vision articulated here. A transformed mental health care system must be results oriented, innovative, consumer focused, well funded, and committed to change.

The clouds of change are already on the horizon, and that perfect storm (or tipping point) of visionary leadership, economic imperative, and public outcry just may hit sooner than we think. If so, this will be the time to move beyond the centuries of stigma, confusion, and heartache that surround mental disorders. This will be the time to create something beautiful on behalf of those who carry such heavy burdens and in so doing to settle something important about who we are and what we stand for. America is a strong and proud nation that has accomplished amazing feats in our short history. Our economic and military powers are currently second to none, and our arts and culture have global impact. But how do we treat those among us for whom the American dream is just an illusion? How hard do we work to make sure that our society is a wonderful place of opportunity not only for the majority but also for those with special challenges such as serious mental illness? History will rightly judge us based not just on our might but on how we treat the more vulnerable among us.

The nation that found independence in the 1700s by unexpectedly defeating the world's superpower, that held together against all odds through a devastating civil war in the 1800s, and that helped defeat world totalitarianism three times in the 1900s can do this. We can decide to roll up our sleeves and create something new—an outcome-oriented, consumer-driven, community-based, innovative, and accountable mental health care system—one that leads to recovery for persons with serious mental illness. We can do what it takes so that those among us who must live their lives with mental disorders can have a real home, a fulfilling job, and deep relationships. We can do what it takes so that our friends and neighbors with serious mental illness can come home.

Postscript—Information on Mental Illness

THERE ARE TWO sources of information for people with mental illness and their families that, in my opinion, outshine the rest. Both are Web sites. Whether one is looking for basic understanding about a particular mental disorder, the latest in treatment options, how to connect with others with similar needs, or books and articles on mental illness, these Web sites can help. Both are excellent and should be browsed by anyone wanting further information on mental illness.

The first is the Web site for the Substance Abuse and Mental Health Services Administration, one of the nation's two federal mental health agencies: www.samhsa.gov. See especially the sections on the left of the home page titled "Treatment Locators" and "Browse by Topic."

The second is the Web site for the National Alliance on Mental Illness, perhaps the nation's most comprehensive and effective mental health advocacy organization: www.nami.org. See especially the subheadings at the top of the home page titled "Inform Yourself" and "Find Support."

Notes

Chapter 1

1. Though the 2007b reference is primarily about the Chinese mental health system, it discusses the U.S. system as well.

2. These are treatments that have received clear research support (Comer 2004).

3. Some policy makers prefer the word *transformation* and others *reform.* These terms are used interchangeably throughout this book, since the basic idea in either case is that it is time for radical change. As for the word *recovery,* its use is not meant to imply that complete healing is possible for serious mental illnesses. In most cases, some aspects of the illness and/or a vulnerability to relapse will remain even with effective treatment. But the recovery model holds that with effective treatment a person suffering from a serious mental illness should be able to function well in his or her home community, with a real home, a fulfilling job, and deep relationships. Thus the "recovery" is of life functioning, not of perfect health.

4. The term *mental health provider* refers to all professionals who provide clinical services for persons with serious mental illness, including psychiatrists, psychologists, social workers, mental health workers, and so on. *Consumers* is a term often used to refer to those who receive services from the mental health care system. Other terms such as *patients* or *clients* are also frequently used. These terms are used interchangeably throughout this book.

5. The reader should note that mental health epidemiological statistics vary greatly depending on the criteria used (e.g., all levels of mental illness, moderate to severe, or only serious mental illness). The figure quoted here includes any and all classifications of mental illness and all levels of severity.

6. See their Web site at www.nami.org.

7. The category referred to is "severe and persistent mental illness," which is conceptually close to serious mental illness.

8. *Tardive dyskinesia* refers to a variety of involuntary, repetitive movements that come as a side effect of long-term or high-dose use of dopamine antagonists such as antipsychotic medications. It is characterized by repetitive, involuntary, purposeless movements such as grimacing, tongue protrusion, lip smacking, rapid movements of the arms, etc. Unfortunately, in many cases it is irreversible.

9. Most first responders in America are trained to offer critical incident stress management (CISM) to disaster survivors who are at risk for PTSD, which involves recounting the trauma in detail. Unfortunately, the research clearly shows that this treatment is not particularly helpful for many and is even harmful for some (see Kelly 2007a). This is a good example of why it is so important to offer only evidence-based treatments for those in need of mental health services.

10. Home and community services should constitute the core components of an effective mental health service delivery system, and the vast majority of persons with serious mental illness should never have to be hospitalized. However, there will always be some who need inpatient care, so there will always be a place for psychiatric hospitals (or hospital wings)—just far fewer than what we currently have.

11. What about persons struggling with autism, mental retardation, or dementia (such as Alzheimer's)? These needs are best addressed in the context of long-term-care support services, as opposed to services focused on serious mental illness.

12. A growing scientific literature demonstrates a link between positive aspects of faith and spirituality and mental health. See, for example, Kelly (2007a).

Chapter 2

1. *Units of service* refers to a discrete treatment or benefit that is separately billed to a funding source such as Medicaid. For instance, a weekly meeting with a counselor for psychotherapy, a monthly meeting with a case manager for problem solving, or a quarterly meeting with a psychiatrist for medication management would all be considered discrete and billable units of service.

2. The science involved is known as either efficacy research, which is performed under controlled situations (usually through a university lab), or effectiveness research, which is performed in the field. Effectiveness research is more applicable, since it takes into account the multiple variables providers must address when working with actual patients in the field. For instance, many patients have more than one diagnosis—such as depression and alcohol dependence—whereas efficacy research focuses on only one diagnosis at a time.

3. A meta-analytic study is one that statistically combines the findings from many single outcome studies on a given treatment, thus producing a grand finding that reflects the entire research literature to date.

4. Of course, there are some exceptions to this rule. Some consumers may be incapable of accurate assessment because of severity of illness, hypochondria, having another agenda requiring the need to "fake bad," etc. In those cases common sense requires relying more heavily on the provider's assessment.

5. The Beck Depression Inventory is a frequently used outcome measure for depression (A. Beck et al. 1961).

6. The Treatment Outcome Package is a thirty-seven-item instrument for measuring adolescent and adult clinical status that meets all scientific criteria (Kraus, Seligman, and Jordan 2005). It is designed to be appropriate for anything from solo practice to large networks of providers and takes approximately twenty minutes for the client to complete. The items primarily cover four areas of concern: depression, anxiety disorders, suicidality, and violence. It is available from Behavioral Health Labs (see www.bhealthlabs.com). The CORE Outcome Measure has thirty-four items designed to measure common symptoms, subjective well-being, life/social functioning, and risk to self and others, and is scientifically sound (Barkham et al. 2001). The instrument is designed to generate a "global level of distress" that is calculated as the mean score of all thirty-four items. This mean score, as well as individual items, can be tracked over the course of therapy as measures of clinical improvement. The measure was developed in England by Britain's Department of Health and has been in use there since 1998 (see CORE System Group 1998 and the group's Web site at www.coreims.co.uk).

7. This was one of three interrelated pilots. The others involved "Priority Populations and Case Rate Funding," designed to test flexible person-centered funding, and "Consumer and Family Development and Participation," designed to increase consumer and family involvement in mental health policy making.

8. The ADA was designed to enable Americans with disabilities to have access to the full range of opportunities society offers. So for example, employers may not discriminate on the basis of disability, and public buildings and sidewalks must be wheelchair accessible.

9. The bottom line improves when waste is rooted out. In this case waste consists of ineffective mental health care.

Chapter 3

1. Many state mental health agencies contract with private sector providers for various services, so they are technically not monopolies, in that they do not own or run the whole show. However, contracting is typically done in a restricted manner that is driven more by agency regulations than by market forces (e.g., finding only one provider per service category), which means that the benefits of an open competitive market are lost. Thus government agencies are monopolistic, even if not quite full monopolies.

2. This term is used here to describe how an organization ceases to focus on its original mission (e.g., serving those with serious mental illness) and instead focuses on self-preservation (e.g., increasing administrative funding and job security). An example of acceptance of poor performance is that many government agencies have inflated employee annual performance reviews in which all concerned expect to be rated as "exceeding expectations" whether or not they do. As commissioner, I instructed my senior executives to use "meets expectations"

for average employees and to save higher ratings for those who really deserved it. This made performance reviews more meaningful and also made high ratings more valuable for those who earned them.

3. These cases are drawn from my own professional experience, either directly or indirectly, but they blend and vary identifying information so that no actual individuals may be recognized.

4. A good place to start such research is www.nami.org.

5. This is typically part of the criteria for admission to a state psychiatric facility. Thankfully, increasing numbers of drug and alcohol programs do not have this requirement for admission.

6. Several states are currently experimenting with this voucher concept, as is SAMHSA.

7. When a mental health agency is seeking a contractor to provide services, it will typically issue a "Request for Proposal," meaning that any potential contractor must submit a detailed written proposal showing exactly what will be provided, and at what cost. The proposal must be in the exact format stipulated by the state and must arrive before deadline. The state then reviews all submissions and selects one or more for contracting.

Chapter 4

1. See "Ohio, New York Governors Sign Mental Health Parity Bills," *Medical News Today*, January 5, 2007, www.medicalnewstoday.com/articles/60157.php.

2. Ibid.

3. The full text of the law can be accessed at http://thomas.loc.gov (search HR 1424).

4. Of course, for this to hold true, insurers must get beyond the tendency to focus only on next quarter's profits and short-term contracts.

Chapter 5

1. The same can be said for many medical/surgical patients, but that is a topic for another book.

2. Psychologists cannot prescribe medications, so they usually collaborate with a psychiatrist or other MD—in this case the clinic MD—when necessary.

3. Psychoanalytic treatment focuses on one's "psychosexual" stages of development per Sigmund Freud and involves bringing unconscious thoughts and impulses to conscious awareness.

4. "Resistance" from the psychoanalytic perspective is defined as "anything that works against the progress of therapy and prevents the client from producing previously unconscious material" (Corey 2001, 94).

5. See discussion of PACT in chapter 2.

6. A case in point is the shooter at Virginia Technological Institute in Blacksburg, Virginia, who killed thirty-two students on April 16, 2007.

7. This is only one scenario for outpatient commitment. State laws and actual applications vary.

8. Psychotropic medications are medications used to treat mental illnesses. They affect the mind, emotions, and behavior (e.g., antidepressants such as Zoloft; antipsychotics such as Risperdal).

9. It is true that some of the most severe and debilitating forms of serious mental illness preclude functioning well in the home community and require either inpatient services or intensive outpatient residential care. But thankfully most people with serious mental illness respond well to effective community care.

10. See chapter 2 for a detailed discussion of these three areas and how to measure them.

11. The Center for Mental Health Services (CMHS)—part of SAMHSA.

12. A medication that makes an individual acutely sensitive to alcohol and thus may help overcome alcoholism.

Chapter 6

1. Virginia operates sixteen psychiatric facilities: seven mental health facilities, five mental retardation training centers, a psychiatric facility for children and adolescents, a medical center for psychiatric patients, a psychiatric geriatric hospital, and a center for behavioral rehabilitation.

2. These are good policies but have been poorly implemented. Nobody should have to live in a psychiatric hospital if anything less restrictive would work. However, many discharged today to community services do not find effective care and end up either on the street or rehospitalized.

3. Generated by Proposition 63, the Mental Health Services Act, which was passed in November 2004. The funds come from a 1 percent tax on taxable income over $1 million.

4. As set by the 1980 Civil Rights for Institutionalized Persons Act (CRIPA).

5. Many stakeholders ultimately need to be at the table for mental health reform. Here is a partial list: mental health service providers and organizations, consumers and family members, federal/state/local legislators and executive branch leaders, hospitals and doctors, private insurance companies and federal insurers such as Medicaid, pharmaceutical companies, big and small businesses, long-term care organizations, relevant unions, law enforcement and judicial branch representatives, and banks and financial/consulting organizations who may be involved in financing health care.

6. This is meant to suggest not that persons with serious mental illness can be cured but that most can be helped to return successfully to their home community—to have a fulfilling job, a real home, and deep relationships. Recovery means successfully integrating a mental disorder into a consumer's overall lifestyle, enabling him or her to have a full, productive life and thereby to minimize dependence on the service system.

References

American Psychiatric Association. 1980. *Diagnostic and statistical manual of mental disorders.* 3rd ed. Washington, DC: American Psychiatric Association.
———. 2000. *Diagnostic and statistical manual of mental disorders, 4th edition, text revision.* Washington, DC: American Psychiatric Press.
Barkham, M., C. Evans, F. Margison, G. McGrath, J. Mellor-Clark, D. Milne, et al. 1998. The rationale for developing and implementing core batteries in service settings and psychotherapy outcome research. *Journal of Mental Health* 7:35–47.
Barkham, M., F. Margison, C. Leach, M. Lucock, J. Mellor-Clark, C. Evans, et al. 2001. Service profile and benchmarking using the CORE-OM: Toward practice-based evidence in the psychological therapies. *Journal of Consulting and Clinical Psychology* 69:184–96.
Beck, A. T., C. H. Ward, M. Mendelson, J. Mock, and J. Erbaugh. 1961. An inventory for measuring depression. *Archives of General Psychiatry* 4:561–71.
Beck, J. S. 1995. *Cognitive therapy: Basics and beyond.* New York: Guilford Press.
Bickman, L. 2005. A common factors approach to improving mental health services. *Mental Health Services Research* 7:1–4.
Blank, M. B., J. R. Koch, and B. J. Burkett. 2004. Less is more: Virginia's Performance Outcomes Measurement System. *Psychiatric Services* 55:643–45.
Borkovec, T. D., R. J. Echemendia, S. A. Ragusea, and M. Ruiz. 2001. The Pennsylvania Practice Research Network and future possibilities for clinically meaningful and scientifically rigorous psychotherapy effectiveness research. *Journal of Mental Health* 10:241–51.
Brower, L. A. 2003. The Ohio Mental Health Consumer Outcome System: Reflections on a major policy initiative in the US. *Clinical Psychology and Psychotherapy* 10:400–406.
Burgess, P., J. Pirkis, and T. Coombs. 2006. Do adults in contact with Australia's public sector mental health services get better? *Australia and New Zealand Health Policy* 3:3–9.
Clarke, M., and A. D. Oxman. 1999. Cochrane reviewers' handbook 4.0 [updated July 1999]. In Review Manager [computer program], Version 4.0. Oxford: Cochrane Collaboration.
Collins, J. 2001. *Good to great.* New York: HarperCollins.

Comer, R. J. 2004. *Abnormal psychology*. New York: Worth.

Corcoran, K., and J. Fischer. 2000. *Measures for clinical practice: A sourcebook*. 3rd ed. 2 vols. New York: Free Press.

CORE System Group. 1998. *CORE System (information management) handbook*. Leeds: CORE System Group.

Corey, G. 2001. *Theory and practice of counseling and psychotherapy*. Belmont, CA: Wadsworth.

Corrigan, P. W., S. G. McCracken, and C. McNeilly. 2005. Evidence-based practices for people with serious mental illness and substance abuse disorders. In *The evidence-based practice: Methods, models, and tools for mental health*, ed. C. E. Stout and R. A. Hayes, 153–56. New York: John Wiley.

Craighead, W. E., D. J. Miklowitz, and L. W. Craighead, eds. 2008. *Psychopathology: History, diagnosis, and empirical foundations*. Hoboken, NJ: John Wiley.

Davies, H., S. Nutley, and P. Smith. 2000. *What works? Evidence-based practice in public services*. Bristol: Policy Press.

DePree, M. 2004. *Leadership is an art*. New York: Doubleday.

Devilly, G. J., R. Gist, and P. Cotton. 2006. Ready! Fire! Aim! The status of psychological debriefing and therapeutic interventions: In the work place and after disasters. *Review of General Psychology* 10:318–45.

Dixon, L. B., and H. H. Goldman. 2003. Forty years of progress in community mental health: The role of evidence-based practice. *Australia and New Zealand Journal of Psychiatry* 37:668–73.

Dohrenwend, B. P., J. B. Turner, N. A. Turse, B. G. Adams, K. C. Koen, and R. Marshall. 2006. The psychological risk of Vietnam for U.S. veterans: A revisit with new data and methods. *Science* 313: 979–82.

Drake, R. E. 1998. Brief history, current status, and future place of assertive community treatment. *American Journal of Orthopsychiatry* 68:172–75.

Drake, R. E., M. Merrens, and D. Lynde, eds. 2005. *Evidence-based mental health: A textbook*. New York: John Wiley.

Drucker, P. F. 2003. *Peter Drucker on the profession of management*. Boston: Harvard Business School Press.

Elkin, I. 1994. The NIMH treatment of depression collaborative research program: Where we began and where we are. In *Handbook of psychotherapy and behavior change*, ed. A. E. Bergin and S. L. Garfield, 4th ed., 114–39. New York: John Wiley.

Emanuel, E., and V. R. Fuchs. 2005. Health care vouchers: A proposal for universal coverage. *New England Journal of Medicine* 352:1255–60.

Engel, G. L. 1977. The need for a new medical model: A challenge for biomedicine. *Science* 196:129–36.

Evans, C., J. Mellor-Clark, F. Margison, M. Barkham, G. McGrath, J. Connell, et al. 2000. Clinical outcomes in routine evaluation: The CORE-OM. *Journal of Mental Health* 9:247–55.

Foley, H. A., and S. S. Scharfstein. 1983. *Madness and government: Who cares for the mentally ill.* Arlington, VA: American Psychiatric Publishing.

Ford, W. E. 1998. Economic grand rounds: Medical necessity: Its impact in managed mental health care. *Psychiatric Services* 49:183–84.

Gladwell, M. 2000. *The tipping point: How little things can make a big difference.* Boston: Back Bay Publishing.

Glicken, M. D. 2004. *Improving the effectiveness of the helping professions: An evidence-based practice approach.* Thousand Oaks, CA: Sage Publications.

Goodwin, C. J. 1999. *A history of modern psychology.* New York: John Wiley.

Gottesman, I. I. 1991. *Schizophrenia genesis: The origins of madness.* New York: W. H. Freeman.

Grob, G. N., and H. H. Goldman. 2006. *The dilemma of federal mental health policy.* New Brunswick: Rutgers University Press.

———. 2007. *The dilemma of federal mental health policy: Radical reform or incremental change?* New Brunswick: Rutgers University Press.

Haas-Wilson, D. 2003. *Managed care and monopoly power: The antitrust challenge.* Cambridge, MA: Harvard University Press.

Harrison, B. M. 2002. Mental health parity. *Harvard Journal on Legislation* 39:255–79.

Health Care for the Homeless Clinicians' Network. 2004. Adapting your practice: General recommendations for the care of homeless patients. www.nhchc.org/Publications/6.1.04GenHomelessRecsFINAL.pdf.

Healy, D. 2004. *Let them eat Prozac: The unhealthy relationship between the pharmaceutical industry and depression.* New York: New York University Press.

Hillman, J. L. 2002. *Crisis intervention and trauma: New approaches to evidence-based practices.* New York: Kluwer Academic/Plenum.

Institute of Medicine. 2006. *Improving the quality of health care for mental health and substance-use conditions.* Washington, DC: National Academies Press.

Jacobson, N. S., L. J. Roberts, S. B. Berns, and J. B. McGlinchey. 1999. Methods for defining and determining the clinical significance of treatment effects: Description, application, and alternatives. *Journal of Consulting and Clinical Psychology* 67:300–307.

Kelly, T. A. 1997. A wake up call: The experience of a mental health commissioner in times of change. *Professional Psychology: Research and Practice* 28:317–22.

———. 2000. Principled mental health system reform. *Heritage Foundation Backgrounder* 1341 (January 7): 1–12.

———. 2002a. *Dealing with fragmentation in the service delivery system.* Invited expert testimony presented to the President's New Freedom Commission on Mental Health, Arlington, VA, December. www.mentalhealthcommission.gov/presentations/presentations.html.

Kelly, T. A. 2002b. A policymaker's guide to mental illness. *Heritage Foundation Backgrounder* 1522 (March 7): 1–16.

———. 2003a. Clinical outcome measurement: A call to action. *Journal of Psychology and Christianity* 22:254–58.

———. 2003b. Transforming the mental health system: Principles and recommendations. Paper presented at the annual meeting of the American Psychological Association, August 10, Toronto.

———. 2007a. The role of religion, spirituality, and faith-based community in coping with acts of terrorism. In *Psychology of terrorism*, ed. B. Bongar, L. M. Brown, L. E. Beutler, J. N. Breckenridge, and P. G. Zimbardo, 137–52. New York: Oxford University Press.

———. 2007b. Transforming China's mental health system: Principles and recommendations. *International Journal of Mental Health* 36:50–64.

Kelly, T. A., and H. H. Strupp. 1992. Patient and therapist values in psychotherapy: Perceived changes, assimilation, similarity, and outcome. *Journal of Consulting and Clinical Psychology* 60:34–40.

Kessler, R. C., P. Berglund, O. Demler, R. Jin, K. R. Merikangas, and E. E. Walters. 2005. Lifetime prevalence and age-of-onset distributions of *DSM-IV* disorders in the National Comorbidity Survey Replication. *Archives of General Psychiatry* 62:593–602.

Kessler, R. C., W. T. Chiu, O. Demler, and E. E. Walters. 2005. Prevalence, severity, and co-morbidity of twelve-month *DSM-IV* disorders in the National Comorbidity Survey Replication (NCS-R). *Archives of General Psychiatry* 62:617–27.

Kohn, L. T., J. M. Corrigan, and M. S. Donaldson, eds. 2000. *To err is human: Building a safer health system.* Washington DC: Institute of Medicine.

Kraus, D. R., D. A. Seligman, and J. R. Jordan. 2005. Validation of a behavioral health treatment outcome and assessment tool designed for naturalistic settings: The Treatment Outcome Package. *Journal of Clinical Psychology* 61:285–314.

Kulka, R. A., et al. 1988. *National Vietnam Veterans Readjustment Study (NVVRS).* Washington, DC: Veterans Administration.

Lambert, M. J., N. B. Hansen, and A. E. Finch. 2001. Patient-focused research: Using patient outcome data to enhance treatment effects. *Journal of Consulting and Clinical Psychology* 69:159–72.

Langewitz, W., M. Nübling, and H. Weber. 2006. Hospital patients' preferences for involvement in decision-making. *Swiss Medical Weekly* 136:59–64.

Lipman-Blumen, J. 1996. *The connective edge.* San Francisco: Jossey-Bass.

Manderscheid, R. 1998. Addressing the crisis of quality in behavioral health care at the millennium. *Journal of Behavioral Health Services and Research* 25:233–36.

————. 1999. Untangling the accountability maze: Developing outcome measures, report cards and performance indicators. *Managed Behavioral Health News,* April, 6–7.

McEvoy, J. P., J. A. Lieberman, T. S. Stroup, S. M. Davis, H. Y. Meltzer, R. A. Rosenheck, M. S. Swartz, et al., for the CATIE Investigators. 2006. Effectiveness of clozapine versus olanzapine, quetiapine, and risperidone in patients with chronic schizophrenia who did not respond to prior atypical antipsychotic treatment. *American Journal of Psychiatry* 163:600–610.

Mechanic, D. 2006. *The truth about health care: Why reform is not working in America.* New Brunswick: Rutgers University Press.

————. 2008. *Mental health and social policy: Beyond managed care.* 5th ed. Boston: Allyn and Bacon.

Meichenbaum, D. 1977. *Cognitive-behavior modification.* New York: Plenum.

Mental Health Statistics Improvement Program [MHSIP] Task Force. 1996. *The Mental Health Statistics Improvement Program Consumer-Oriented Mental Health Report Card.* Rockville, MD: Center for Mental Health Services.

Merrens, M. 2005. *Evidence-based mental health practice.* New York: W. W. Norton.

Miranda, J., J. Y. Chung, and B. L. Green. 2003. Treating depression in predominantly low-income minority women: A randomized controlled trial. *Journal of the American Medical Association* 290:57–65.

Muris, T. J. 2002. *Everything old is new again: Health care and competition in the 21st century.* Washington, DC: U.S. Federal Trade Commission.

Murray, C. J., and A. D. Lopez. 1996. Evidence-based health policy: Lessons from the Global Burden of Disease Study. *Science* 274:740–43.

Nathan, P. E., and J. M. Gorman, eds. 2002. *A guide to treatments that work.* 2nd ed. New York: Oxford University Press.

National Alliance on Mental Illness. 2008. About mental illness. www.nami.org/ Content/NavigationMenu/Inform_Yourself/About_Mental_Illness/ About_Mental_Illness.htm.

National Alliance to End Homelessness. 2000. *A plan, not a dream: How to end homelessness in ten years.* Washington, DC: National Alliance to End Homelessness.

National Association of State Mental Health Program Directors [NASMHPD] Research Institute. 1998. *Five state feasibility study on state mental health agency performance measures.* June. Prepared for U.S. Center for Mental Health Services. Alexandria, VA: National Association of State Mental Health Program Directors Research Institute.

National Institute of Mental Health. 2000. *Treatment of children with mental disorders.* NIH Pub. No. 00-4702. Bethesda, MD: National Institutes of Health.

————. 2007. *Anxiety disorders.* NIH Pub. No. 06-3879. Bethesda, MD: National Institutes of Health.

Newhouse, J. P. 1999. *Health insurance experiment in metropolitan and non-metropolitan areas of the United States, 1974–1982.* Santa Monica, CA: Rand Corporation.

Office of Technology Assessment. 1994. *Identifying health technologies that work: Searching for evidence.* Pub. No. OTA-H-608, September. Washington, DC: Government Printing Office.

Office of the Surgeon General. 1999. *Mental health: A report of the surgeon general.* Rockville, MD: U.S. Department of Health and Human Services.

Olson, R. P. 2006. Mental health systems compared: Great Britian, Norway, Canada, and the United States. Springfield, IL: Charles C. Thomas.

Pirkis, J., P. Burgess, T. Coombs, A. Clarke, D. Jones-Ellis, and R. Dickson. 2005. Routine measurement of outcomes in Australian public sector mental health services. *Australia and New Zealand Health Policy* 11:20–27.

President's New Freedom Commission on Mental Health. 2002. *Interim report to the president.* Rockville, MD: President's New Freedom Commission on Mental Health.

———. 2003. *Achieving the promise: Transforming mental health care in America.* Rockville, MD: President's New Freedom Commission on Mental Health. DHHS Pub. No. SMA-03-3832.

Prochaska, J. O., and J. C. Norcross. 2003. *Systems of psychotherapy: A transtheoretical analysis.* 5th ed. Pacific Grove, CA: Brooks/Cole.

Rosenbach, M., et al. 2003. *Effects of the Vermont Mental Health and Substance Abuse Parity Law.* DHHS Pub. No. (SMA) 03-3822. Rockville, MD: Center for Mental Health Services, Substance Abuse and Mental Health Services Administration.

Rosenberg, L. 2008. Mental health and substance use care in the 2008 election. Paper presented at the annual American College of Mental Health Administration summit, March, Santa Fe.

Rosenstein, M. J., and L. J. Millazzo-Sayre. 1981. *Characteristics of admissions to selected mental health facilities.* DHHS Pub. ADM 931005. Washington, DC: Government Printing Office.

Roth, A., and P. Fonagy. 1996. *What works for whom? A critical review of psychotherapy research.* New York: Guilford Press.

Sabin, J., and N. Daniels. 1994. Determining "medical necessity" in mental health practice. *Hastings Center Report* 214:5–13.

Seligman, M. 1994. *What you can change and what you can't.* New York: Knopf.

———. 1995. The effectiveness of psychotherapy. *American Psychologist* 50:965–74.

Shadish, W. R., A. M. Navarro, G. E. Matt, and G. Phillips. 2000. The effects of psychological therapies under clinically representative conditions: A meta-analysis. *Psychological Bulletin* 126:512–29.

Smith, M., G. Glass, and T. Miller. 1980. *The benefit of psychotherapy.* Baltimore: Johns Hopkins University Press.

Stanbury, W., and F. Thompson. 1995. Toward a political economy of government waste: First step, definitions. *Public Administration Review* 55:418–27.

Stroup, T. S., J. A. Lieberman, J. P. McEvoy, M. S. Swartz, S. M. Davis, R. A. Rosenheck, D. O. Perkins, et al., for the CATIE Investigators. 2006. Effectiveness of olanzapine, quetiapine, risperidone and ziprasidone in patients with chronic schizophrenia following discontinuation of a previous atypical antipsychotic. *American Journal of Psychiatry* 163:611–22.

Substance Abuse and Mental Health Services Administration. 2003a. Children's mental health facts: Children and adolescents with anxiety disorders. http://mentalhealth.samhsa.gov/publications/allpubs/ca-0007/default.asp.

———. 2003b. *State and county psychiatric hospitals, inpatient census, end of 2000.* Rockville, MD: U.S. Department of Health and Human Services.

———. 2006. Suicidal thoughts, suicide attempts, major depressive episode, and substance use among adults. *OAS Report* 34:1–8.

———. 2007. *Results from the 2006 National Survey on Drug Use and Health: National findings.* Office of Applied Studies, NSDUH Series H-32, DHHS Pub. No. SMA 07-4293. Rockville, MD: U.S. Department of Health and Human Services.

Tan, S., and J. Ortberg. 2004. *Coping with depression.* Grand Rapids, MI: Baker Books.

Whiteford, H. A., and W. J. Buckingham. 2005. Ten years of mental health service reform in Australia: Are we getting it right? *Medical Journal of Australia* 182:396–400.

World Health Organization. 2003. *Advocacy for mental health.* Geneva: World Health Organization.

———. 2004. *The World Health Report 2004: Changing history.* Geneva: World Health Organization.

Index

AA. *See* Alcoholics Anonymous (AA)
Achieving the Promise (President's New Freedom Commission on Mental Health), 115, 139
ACT. *See* Assertive Community Treatment (ACT)
ADA. *See* Americans with Disabilities Act (ADA, 1990)
ADHD. *See* attention deficit/hyperactivity disorder (ADHD)
"adverse selection" issue, 94–95
Advocacy for Mental Health (World Health Organization), 115
advocacy organizations, 61, 120–122, 126–127, 161
agoraphobia, 13, 20
Alcoholics Anonymous (AA), 25, 78, 137
Allen, George, 2
Americans with Disabilities Act (ADA, 1990), 47, 169n8
anorexia nervosa, 24
anticonvulsants, 19
antidepressants, 18, 39, 44. *See also* selective serotonin reuptake inhibitors (SSRIs)
antipsychotic medications: deinstitutionalization, 62; inpatient care, 8; population in mental hospitals, 8; schizophrenia, 16, 62; side effects, 8, 16; tardive dyskinesia, 167n8
antismoking movement, 148–149
antitrust laws, enforcement of, 85–86

antitrust policy, 65
anxiety disorders: agoraphobia, 13, 20; avoidant behaviors, 20; phobias, 20; psychotherapy, 21–22; recovery for people with, 22; as serious mental illness, 13, 19; symptoms, 19; treatment, 21–22. *See also* obsessive-compulsive disorder; panic disorder; PTSD
Assertive Community Treatment (ACT) effectiveness, 43
asylums, 7–8
attention deficit/hyperactivity disorder (ADHD), 22–23
Australia, clinical outcome measures in, 55–56
autism, 168n11
Aviator (film), 20

A Beautiful Mind (film), 15
Beck Depression (or Anxiety) Inventory, 127, 162, 168n5
behavioral therapy, 23
benzodiazepines, 21
"biologically based mental illnesses," 99
biopsychosocial model of mental illness: acceptance of, 10; biological component, 10; etiology of mental illness, 14; psychological component, 10; social component, 10, 29
bipolar disorder, 13, 18–19
Bleuler, Eugen, 15

mental illness, 107; "sins" of, 107; vicious cycle of discharge and re-hospitalization, 9, 122, 150. *See also* inpatient care
Hughes, Howard, 20

iCan, 71
inpatient care: antipsychotic medications, 8; clinical outcome measures, 42, 45, 55; post-traumatic stress disorder (PTSD), 8; rise of, 8. *See also* hospitalization for mental illness
Institute of Medicine, 131
insurance industry: "adverse selection" issue, 94–95; annual or lifetime spending limits, 94; capitated systems, 108; clinical outcome measures, 32, 52–54, 61–62, 155; cost sharing, 94, 95; employer-sponsored health insurance, 101; evidence-based practices, 44; fee-for-service systems, 108; initial visits, coverage for, 82; marketing of services, 62; medical necessity, 104; "moral hazard" issue, 94–95, 109; parity (*see* parity coverage for mental health); preferred providers, 77, 83; premiums, increase in, 146; reform of the mental health system, 32; resistance to transformation of mental health system, 142; responsibilities in transforming the mental health system, 155; self-insured plans, 101; severity of illness, 13; shifting of mental health costs to the public sector, 79; "shopping around" for providers, 82–83; support for innovative mental health care, 61
Interim Report to the President (President's New Freedom Commission on Mental Health), 1

interpersonal psychotherapy, 39, 44, 81

Kaiser/Community Health Plan, 98
Kennedy, John F., 132

leadership. *See* visionary leadership
less severe mental health needs, 29–31, 152
Lincoln, Abraham, 1
lithium, 19
long-term support services, 168n11
Lynchburg Training Center (Virginia), 3–4, 27. *See also* Central Virginia Training Center

major depressive disorder: Alison (a patient), 116–118; antidepressants, 18; caffeine intoxication compared to, 12, 96; cognitive-behavioral psychotherapy, 81, 117–118; Evelyn (a patient), 80–81; interpersonal psychotherapy, 81; Jon (a patient), 92–93; outcome measure for, 168n5; overmedication, 18, 116–117; psychosocial stressors, 17; self-harm, 18, 92–93, 116; suicide, 17, 92; symptoms, 17; treatment, 17–18; weight gain, 116–117
Managed Care and Monopoly Power (Haas-Wilson), 65, 72–73
manic depression. *See* bipolar disorder
Martz, Michael, 140
Mary (a patient's wife), 135–138
mathematics disorder, 13
Mechanic, David, 139
Medicaid, 69, 95, 146–147, 168n1
medical necessity: clinical necessity compared to, 159; parity coverage for mental health, 103–109; replacement by clinical necessity, 109, 112, 159

recovery for people with serious
mental illness: *Achieving the Promise* (President's New Freedom
Commission on Mental Health),
139; anxiety disorders, 22; clinical outcome measures, 38–39, 59;
community mental health centers
(CMHCs), 62–63; collaborative
mental health, 127; definition of
recovery, 48–49; focuses of, 39;
functional life improvement, 39; future envisioned, 139; goal of mental
health treatment, 106; possibility
of, 14; President's New Freedom
Commission on Mental Health on,
6; from schizophrenia, 16; services
and support necessary for, 62–63;
symptom reduction, 39; transformation of the mental health system,
6; vicious cycle of discharge and
rehospitalization, 9, 122, 150
"recovery" model of mental health
treatment, 106, 167n3
recovery-oriented care, 48–49
reform, use of the term, 167n3
reform of the mental health system: incremental approaches to, 140, 142;
insurance industry, 32; integration
of health care and mental health
care systems, 130–134; stakeholders in, 171n5; uninsured people,
160; universal health care, 160
relapse in substance use disorders, 26
relapse prevention, 107, 109
religious institutions in mental health
treatment, 31, 152
Roosevelt, Theodore, 88

SAMHSA. *See* Substance Abuse and
Mental Health Services Administration (SAMHSA)
schizophrenia: antipsychotic

medications, 16, 62; definition, 15;
emotional responses of persons
with, 16; hearing voices not there,
9, 15, 74; overmedication, 75; prevalence, 15; recovery from, 16; as
serious mental illness, 9; Susan (a
patient), 74–76; symptoms, 15–16;
treatment, 16–17; types, 15
schools in mental health treatment,
30–31, 152
seasonal affective disorder, 105
selective serotonin reuptake inhibitors
(SSRIs), 18, 21–22, 44
self-advocacy, 126, 161–162
self-harm: major depressive disorder,
18, 92–93, 116; mental illness, 1
Seligman, Martin, 39
serious mental illness, 11–29; bases of,
12; "biologically based mental illnesses," 100; categories of, 12–13;
definition, 11–13, 96–97, 100, 152;
diagnosis in, 12; *DSM-IV,* 11–12;
early intervention programs, 14;
functioning in home community,
171n9; hallmark of, 97; hospitalization for, 107; level of functioning
in, 12, 13; National Alliance for
the Mentally Ill (NAMI), 11, 12;
percent of American adults suffering from, 97; prevalence, 13;
prevention of, 14; prioritization of,
11–12, 29–30, 96, 113; psychiatric
facility care, 26–29; recovery from
(*see* recovery for people with serious mental illness); substance use
disorders, co-occurrence with, 13,
24–25; symptoms and treatment of
common disorders, 14–26
specialization, 75
SSRIs. *See* selective serotonin reuptake
inhibitors (SSRIs)
stakeholders, 171n5

About the Author

DR. TIMOTHY A. KELLY currently directs the DePree Public Policy Institute (www.depree.org) and served as commissioner of Virginia's Department of Mental Health from 1994 to 1997.